Economics for the Construction Industry

R C Shutt
MCIOB, BA

Economics for the Construction Industry

Third Edition

 LONGMAN

Addison Wesley Longman Limited
Edinburgh Gate, Harlow
Essex CM20 2JE, England
and Associated Companies throughout the world.

First published 1982
Second edition 1988
Reprinted 1989, 1990, 1992
Third edition 1995
Second impression 1997

British Library Cataloguing in Publication Data
A catalogue entry for this title is available from the British Library

ISBN 0-582-22912-X

Set by 4 in Compugraphic Times 10/11
Produced through Longman Malaysia, TCP

To MEAT 3

Contents

Acknowledgements

The author is grateful to the Controller of Her Majesty's Stationery Office, for permission to reproduce many of the statistics used in this text, from copies of *The Annual Abstract of Statistics*, *Housing and Construction Statistics*, and *The UK National Accounts*.

Thanks are given to the Office for the Official Publications of the European Communities for permission to use extracts from *Europe in figures* from *Eurostat*.

Thanks are also extended to all those who have in any way helped in the production of this publication.

Introduction

This book was written to provide an easily read introductory reference work for construction students on economics units of HNC, HND, degree and CIOB courses. Wherever possible the discussion is put into the context of the construction industry and certain sections are solely concerned with this industry.

Economics can be said to be the satisfaction of wants by the allocation of scarce factors. It is however very difficult, due to the very nature of the subject, to offer a precise definition. Economics, as will be seen, can be applied to all levels, from an individual, through enterprise and government levels, right through to world economics, covering such aspects as scarce world resource allocation.

On an individual level, economic decisions are often accomplished fairly quickly. When national problems are considered, however, the factors to be taken into account are often numerous, complex and inter-related. For these reasons, decisions at this level often come very slowly, and, as has often proved the case, the correct decisions are not made.

The solving of economic problems at the higher levels is not easy; if it was, countries would not face present problems.

A word of advice for the newcomer to the subject. When faced with the various laws and theories, always study the theory on its own first. It should then be applied to a controlled situation, in a similar manner to that in which a controlled scientific experiment is carried out. Only when it is thoroughly understood should it be applied to a real situation where other laws may operate simultaneously.

Students should endeavour to increase their knowledge of the subject, by careful reading and application, not only from text books, but also from good daily newspapers and professional journals. The latter should give a feel for the complexity of real dynamic situations existing today.

It should be borne in mind that economics is not a precise subject, like mathematics or structural engineering. It is a subject where various opinions have to be voiced and where constructive debate should be encouraged, to gain a full understanding of the topics covered.

Chapter 1

The identification of economic resources

Introduction

Although many people might not realise it, everyone is involved in the application of economics in one form or another. Economics is concerned with the satisfying of people's needs or wants by the allocation of scarce resources. As resources are generally limited, whilst people's wants are not, we all have to allocate the resources to cover those wants most urgently needed.

Economics is often studied at two different levels: **microeconomics**, which is concerned with the study of the consumer, households and businesses; **macroeconomics**, which is that part of economics concerned with national or international relationships or theories.

The resources available are better known to economists as factors of production or inputs.

The classification of the inputs into the various categories is often very debatable, and economists' views vary in many instances. The following discussion, however, should give the student some idea of what economists mean by the various factors.

There are three factors that all economists agree are necessary for production, these are land, labour and capital. The fourth category which is regarded by some is the entrepreneurial function. (See Fig. 1.1.)

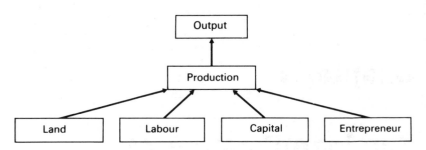

Fig. 1.1 Factors of production

Land

These are the natural resources, used in the production processes. Under this heading could be included such examples as:

(a) Land as it is known under the normal definition, e.g. farmland, woodland storage areas etc.
(b) Water and water areas, e.g. river water, the use of the sea, rivers and canals.
(c) The naturally occurring resources, such as minerals, naturally occurring fuels and chemicals. Also organic natural resources, such as fish, timber, pigs, even crocodiles used for handbags, could be included.
(d) Land has also been defined as a gift of nature, and under this definition could be included wind and water power, and even solar power. The machinery used to extract this energy, however, is classed as capital.

It has often been said that land, as a factor of production, has a finite quantity, meaning that there is only a certain fixed amount available. Is this true? If we consider three main examples of land:

(a) land in the form of actual areas of ground or areas of water
(b) organic resources
(c) inorganic resources

it will be seen that the answer is far from straightforward.

The first group, one might say, is obviously finite, as areas of land cannot be produced or expanded. Or can they?

There are land reclamation schemes, where areas are being recovered from the sea or fenland, or the filling in of worked-out gravel pits, to form farmland. Looking at the other side of the question, there are many coastal regions where erosion of land is taking place, so reducing land areas.

So far, land has been considered as a factor of production, that may be used in the production process as farmland, or for the storing of products during manufacture. If the land is at present completely economically useless, is it still classed as a factor of production? Such an example might be desert land.

Here again opinions differ, one could argue that it is useful for defence training, in that bombers must have somewhere to practise. It all depends upon the wants we wish to satisfy. If the requirement is for food then obviously, with present technology, many desert areas would not be economically viable for food production, and should not be regarded as a factor. If, however, by a massive irrigation scheme the desert could be made fertile, then the stock of agricultural land could be increased.

It can be seen then that the quantity of land areas is not strictly fixed.

The second group, organic resources, is often called renewable resources. These are resources that are possible to replace by biological means, e.g. timber, animals, crops etc. Providing the demand for these resources does not cause extinction, or that pollution does not cause a breakdown in the reproductive cycles, then these resources can be reproduced, so are therefore not finite.

The third group, inorganic resources, also has another name, that of non-renewable resources. This must be qualified by stating that only relatively short time periods are being considered here. This must be emphasised, for given enough time, say a few hundred million years, many minerals may be formed through geological processes. This does, however, depend upon many factors outside our scope.

The statement concerning the fixed quantity of land is more likely to apply to this third group than the other two.

Law of diminishing returns

A discussion on the properties of land areas is often used as a basis for a discussion on the law of diminishing returns.

This law states that successive application of the other inputs to a given amount of a fixed input, will yield proportionately less output/fixed unit of input (productivity) after a certain point. Consider the following example.

A farmer owns a fixed area of land which he wants to make more productive. He does so by adding one extra man at a time, together with additional units of machinery and the necessary supervision. The results are shown in Table 1.1. From this table it can be seen that up to and including the employment of the sixth man the returns are increasing proportionately, and the greatest productivity is when six men are employed. If further labour is added the productivity drops. This is only to be expected, for if it were not the case, a farmer would be able to produce more and more from a given area, by just adding more of the other factors. This is obviously absurd, as the point will eventually be reached where men and machines could not move, due to overcrowding. It is often easier to grasp the situation by showing the productivity of Table 1.1 in the form of a histogram as in Fig. 1.2.

As another example, an owner of a joinery shop wants to increase productivity by putting more men, machines, materials and supervision into the existing premises. The same sort of results would probably occur. The figures would be different but again the situation would give increasing returns initially, followed by diminishing returns.

Table 1.1 Output showing diminishing returns

Labourers	Total output (tonnes)	Productivity output/man	
1	3	3	
2	7	3.5	
3	12	4	Increasing returns
4	18	4.5	
5	25	5	
6	31	5.2	
7	36	5.15	
8	40.5	5.1	Diminishing returns
9	45	5.0	
10	48	4.8	

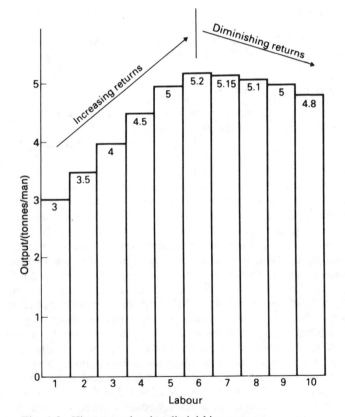

Fig. 1.2 Histogram showing diminishing returns

A nation's land resource

The type of land owned by a country very often dictates, to a certain extent, the type of industry and society that will exist. If the country has very fertile land, then farming may predominate. If it owns vast reserves of minerals, ores and fuels etc. then industry may be the major occupation.

Labour

This is the easiest factor to define, as it is quite simply the skill and effort expended by manpower. Labour, as a factor of production means not only those people who actually help to produce commodities, such as bricklayers or farmworkers, but also those who help to supply a service, for example architects or teachers.

Different criteria affect labour at different levels of investigation.

Labour at enterprise or industry level

The contribution that labour makes at an enterprise or industry level depends upon two main considerations:

1. The relative mix of other factors. For example land, capital and entrepreneurial activities.

In a labour-intensive situation, productivity per man will be much lower than in a capital-intensive situation, assuming an output of similar products. In other words, many more men will need to be employed in a labour-intensive situation, to equal the output of similar products in a capital-intensive situation. The mix of labour and land can be discussed along the lines of Fig. 1.2 concerning increasing and decreasing returns. As was seen earlier, only so much labour can be put on a given area of land, before efficiency decreases.

The organisation of labour is a very important aspect of production: generally, the better a workforce is organised and supervised, the more efficient it is; without the risk-taking element of production, however, there would be no demand for the labour factor.

2. Working conditions. The psychology of human relations and environment plays a great part these days in the personnel function of any enterprise. A worker in a satisfied frame of mind is more content, works better and is less likely to make mistakes. Hence an employer should consider:

(a) general working environment
(b) adequate remuneration
(c) job satisfaction
(d) sports and social facilities, and other benefits
(e) relationships with colleagues

Labour at a national level

Here different points must be considered to determine labour's contribution to the national output.

1. The climate of the country. In a temperate zone, workmen may be able to work for long periods without extremes of temperature tiring them unduly. As an example, imagine the probable outputs from construction workers operating:

(a) in Britain
(b) in Narvik in Norway in the Arctic Circle
(c) in Kenya on the Equator

The output from a similar labour force would obviously be different in the three countries, assuming all aspects other than temperature remain constant.

2. Education and training. These may dictate what type of work a nation's labour force is able to perform. In a nation where there are good educational facilities, the labour force will tend to aim for more complex, skilled jobs, leaving few people to do the more mundane, unskilled work. This tends to be the case in America or Europe. Eventually the situation may arise where the labourers get as much if not more than the foremen, because they are in greater demand.

At the other end of the scale, as was the case in certain less developed countries, labour consisted of virtually a labouring class, through lack of education and training. In these countries it was often necessary to import expert labour in many fields, to help in construction, and many other newly developing industries.

3. Living conditions and standards. Living conditions and a nation's standard of living are generally decided by the level of national output and growth, in comparison with other countries. Living conditions and standards of living are all relative, but a worker who knows he has a good standard of living feels more content than a worker who knows he hasn't. The benefits distributed by the nation in the form of health and welfare can increase output. It could be argued that high State benefits in the form of unemployment or social security sickness payments, may lead to lower output, due to people applying for benefits that they are not entitled to.

4. The population. The total population of a country will obviously affect the amount of production that can take place. This in turn affects GDP (gross domestic product) which in turn is likely to affect potential growth rates.

5. Age distribution. The age distribution of the population together with the total population will show more accurately a country's ability to produce goods. Consider Table 1.2. Countries A and B have the same total population. Country B however has 10 million more workers than country A. Clearly, on purely labour numbers, country B should have a larger output than A.

Table 1.2   Populations

	Country A	Country B
Below working age	10 m.	7 m.
Workers	25 m.	35 m.
Retired and on-workers	15 m.	8 m.
Total	50 m.	50 m.

6. *Optimum population.* The optimum population for a nation is that population which, when combined with the country's other factors of production, yields the greatest output. This of course has to be related to age distribution of the population. If further information is added to Table 1.2 to give Table 1.3 it could be deduced that country B is underpopulated. Underpopulation is said to exist if there should be a larger population to obtain the most efficient production. Overpopulation obviously means the opposite.

Table 1.3   Populations

	Country A	Country B
Working population	25 m.	35 m.
Total population	50 m.	50 m.
Land areas	Small	Large
Resources	Few	Many
Consumption	Small	Large

Types of occupation

The working population of a nation will be distributed over a wide variety of occupations. The types of occupation will show not only the ability to produce certain goods, but also the state of development of the economy of the nation.

Highly developed nations tend to have a greater proportion of their labour force employed in supervisory, clerical and service jobs. An underdeveloped country will have the majority of its workers concerned with the physical production of goods.

Capital

Many words have a completely different meaning when used in economics to that normally understood to be meant in the common language. Capital is one such word, and we will first consider the economic definition as required for the factors of production. Later the accountant's definition will be considered.

Economic capital is often said to be wealth which is used to produce further wealth. A more easily understandable definition may be simply the plant, machinery, raw materials or any other commodity which helps to produce further goods or services. It must be emphasised that in economics it does not mean just money.

Some examples of capital might include: factory premises, sheet steel, plastics, lorries, office furniture, manufacturing plant.

In order to obtain a fixed output of production, it is necessary to maintain the capital items necessary to produce them. A major problem with many capital items is that they wear out or depreciate. Also, certain machines, particularly in the high-technology field, become obsolete. Even though they may function perfectly well, in the interests of efficiency they should be replaced with the next generation of machine, which works faster, or can produce more or better components. In the late 1970s and early 1980s computers were an ideal example of this last case.

Depreciation is generally fairly easy to understand when talking in terms of a depreciating asset. For instance after 3−5 years it is often cheaper to replace a lorry than to keep it and pay out high maintenance costs. A certain figure must be set aside each year to replace the item, not just to have available the amount of money the item cost initially.

Obsolescence, on the other hand, is often very difficult to allow for. Decisions as to when plant is likely to become obsolete are often just educated guesswork.

To maintain a standard of living it is necessary to set aside certain current production, to allow for depreciation of capital goods. If growth in living standards is aimed for, we need capital growth, not just replacement.

(a) To maintain living standards:
      production must equal **consumption + depreciation**
(b) To increase living standards:
      production must equal **consumption + depreciation + capital growth**

This process of adding to capital is known as investment; again, possibly a conflict of definition. A person might say 'I have just invested £10 000 in the bank'. In economic terms this money has not been invested by the individual. The bank, however, might give a loan of £10 000 to a contractor who uses the money to buy a new tower crane. This act would be understood to be economic investment. In economic theory, money by itself is useless. It cannot be used to produce anything. It is its function as a medium of exchange that enables capital equipment to be purchased, and so aid the production process.

Investment then can be said to be the act of increasing capital.

Consider the following situation.

A country has a fixed amount of production output, this output can be varied between goods which can be classed as investment − e.g. lorries, roads, factories, machine tools and office furniture etc. − or goods which can be classed as consumption, e.g. food, cigarettes, private cars, refrigerators and furniture for the home.

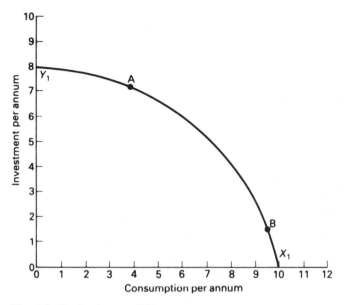

Fig. 1.3 Production possibility curve

Why can furniture be included in both investment and consumption? The reason is this. An armchair if bought for a home would not aid production. The same chair if put into an office could be said to aid the production process albeit only in a minor way.

This splitting of the above country's production into either consumption or investment can best be seen by a production possibility curve which is also known as a transformation curve. (See Fig. 1.3.)

A country can, in theory, choose its output to be anywhere on curve $X_1 Y_1$. However, it is more likely to be between points A and B. If the country chooses it to be between A and Y_1, then this gives a production of many investment goods but few consumption goods. If the choice lies between B and X_1 this gives mainly consumption goods, with few investments goods. Remember that for even a static standard of living, some production must be set aside in the form of investment to allow for depreciation and obsolescence.

For a country to be able to increase its net investment, it must either be able to produce more, or consume less, or be given foreign aid with which to build new factories, irrigation schemes or whatever.

Figure 1.4 illustrates the outcome of two levels of consumption. The first, at point L, gives high consumption with low investment — so low in fact, that it probably would not cover depreciation. This being so, the production possibility curve may diminish to $X_2 Y_2$ in the next production period.

The second, at point M, shows low consumption with high investment. This should lead to an increased production possibility curve $X_3 Y_3$ in the coming production period.

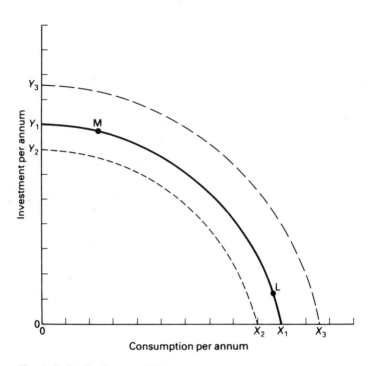

Fig. 1.4 Production possibility curve

Remember:

net investment = gross investment − depreciation and obsolescence losses

If net investment is positive, the production possibility curve will expand. If it is negative, it will contract.

Figures 1.3 and 1.4 allow another concept to be examined, that of opportunity cost.

Opportunity cost

There are many ways of classifying costs. Accountants or estimators may talk of fixed or variable costs, or sometimes direct or indirect costs. Politicians may talk of social costs, but the main concern of economists is opportunity cost.

Opportunity cost may be defined as the cost to the individual, enterprise or whatever, of the alternatives foregone, as a result of a decision to carry out a specific action. Consider the following example. An individual buys a pair of shoes at £40. The opportunity cost to that person, however, may be the new briefcase that he cannot now afford. In this example, the person had £40. He could either buy a pair of shoes, or a briefcase. He chose the shoes, so the cost to him is the briefcase.

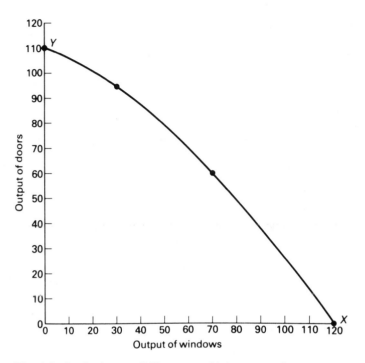

Fig. 1.5   Production possibility curve of joinery manufacture

Consider another example which is concerned with a time cost rather than a value cost. Imagine it is Saturday morning, and Mr Jones has two jobs that he could do. He could either wash the car or dig the garden. If he was to wash the car, the opportunity cost to him would be the fact that he could not now dig the garden.

An example of production at national level was used earlier, where a country may decide to increase investment production, at the cost of consumption (Figs. 1.3 and 1.4). Here the opportunity cost of increasing investment is the lowering of consumption. A similar argument can be applied at enterprise level. (See Fig. 1.5.)

In this simplified example, a joinery manufacturer combines his factors of production, and can produce with them 110 doors or 120 windows, or a combination anywhere along line *XY*. If the manufacturer chooses to produce all doors, the opportunity cost is the windows that can not now be produced.

The entrepreneurial function

This is the risk-taking or organising element of production, and would include the following:

(a) Discovery, recognition and development of profit-making opportunities.
(b) The providing or acquiring of funds for an enterprise.
(c) The organising of the other factors in the optimum proportions in order to make a profit.
(d) The supervision of production.

In Britain during the late eighteenth to early twentieth century, this was the time for the great entrepreneurs. Men who recognised profit-making opportunities, and who organised the factors to gain that profit. During this period, the dual roles of the entrepreneur were nearly always vested in one man, the founder of the firm, the true entrepreneur. As the entrepreneurial function became more and more complex, due to greater union activity, greater State involvement through legislation, and greater competition from abroad, this dual role has tended not to be vested in one man, but in many specialists.

In the average limited company of today, the organising role is usually the ultimate responsibility of a paid manager, who has under him many sub-managers. The major risk-taking role is usually now undertaken by the shareholdes of the company, who supply the money for the managers to purchase factors in order that production can take place. The shareholders risk their money, but the management also takes risks in the organisation of production. Certain risks that are taken are calculable, and as such are often insured against. Such risks may be:

(a) Damage by fire or flood.
(b) Accidents to employees or third parties.
(c) One can even insure against plant becoming obsolete.

There are, however, still many forms of risk that are not calculable. For instance:

(a) A builder may need to order in advance the number of bricks he will require within the next 12 months.
(b) A manufacturer of clothing has to take a chance on what types of garment will be in fashion next season.
(c) Mining companies take great risks when deciding upon what areas to concentrate their exploration.

One key problem concerned with risk-taking is that of time. A manager may make decisions today on the setting up or altering of a process on which goods may not be made for months, or even years. By the time the process is operational, the demand may have altered or even disappeared.

Profit is the payment for the taking of risks, hence the reason many companies put managers on profit-sharing schemes. It will generally be found that where greater potential profits exist, greater risks will be taken to try to acquire these profits. Compare the three examples above in the context of their respective risks.

If the decisions made in the examples in Table 1.4 are correct, the potential

Table 1.4 Potential risks and profits

	Risk	Potential profit
Builder (brick supplies)	Low	Low
Clothing manufacturer (styles)	Medium	Medium
Mining company (exploration areas)	High	High

profit may have been realised. If the wrong decisions are made, the following may happen.

(a) The builder orders too many bricks. He may have to stockpile them until they can be used. His only loss is the interest payable on the money used to buy the stockpiled bricks.
(b) The clothing manufacturer may have to sell off stock cheaply, so that he still gets some income.
(c) The mining company loses its exploration costs, which may be considerable, and gets no income from mineral finds.

Earlier profit was mentioned, but what is normal profit? It can be seen from the above that normal profit would have to take into account the risks involved. Normal profit therefore is that profit required to persuade entrepreneurs to continue in a given enterprise, and is likely to be different for different business activities.

Questions

1 Take an average construction company, put down the four inputs, and list five or six items under each that could be used in the construction process.
2 A quarry owner decides to increase output per machine and invests in more excavating machines, labour etc. Using Fig. 1.2 as a guide, determine at what point diminishing returns set in, using the figures in Table 1.5.

Table 1.5

Number of machines	Total output/ day (tonnes)
2	70
3	110
4	155
5	195
6	220
7	237

3 From Fig. 1.3 over a period of several years, a country has had a consumption of 9 units. This has resulted in curve *XY* not fluctuating from the position shown. If due to government measures, consumption is reduced to 8 units, what is likely to happen in future production periods if the government intervention is removed?

4 Within the context of the construction industry, discuss three different situations for the operation of opportunity cost.

5 As a construction student, why do you think it is necessary to study economics? Write a few brief paragraphs expressing your thoughts at this stage.

Chapter 2

The allocation of resources

Introduction

So far we have considered the various inputs necessary for production. In this chapter we will see how these inputs are distributed according to the many requirements of society.

Why do they need to be distributed, one may ask: surely there are enough resources to go round?

In normal situations, all things are scarce, which in economics means supply is limited relative to demand. Most people would like to own a large house, a fast car or fine clothes etc. but cannot have them at the price they are willing to pay.

Scales of preference

Society, faced with this problem of scarcity, tries to satisfy rationally as many wants as it can within its means. Again, this idea can be interpreted at all levels of society, be it individual, family, business enterprise or nation.

For example, a consumer may have a list of wants such as the following:

(a) television set
(b) replacement car

(c) lawn mower
(d) greenhouse

If these items were in preference order, the consumer would gain the greatest satisfaction from the television. The next greatest satisfaction from exchanging his car for a new one, and so on. This list is particular to the person concerned, as another person's choices may be totally different. These lists are known as scales of preference, and it is the study of such lists which aids the formulation of demand statistics required by entrepreneurs.

Society in general then tries to distribute its resources in such a manner as to give the greatest degree of satisfaction within that society. This may be said to give the greatest standard of living within the prevailing circumstances.

Utility

The ability of a good to satisfy wants is known as its utility. It must be emphasised that in economics, utility does not mean how useful a good is. It was stated earlier that each person has his or her own scale of preference at any one time; therefore a television, for instance, is likely to have a different utility for different people.

From everyday situations it can be deduced that the more a consumer has of a certain good, the slower will be the rate of increase of the total utility the good will give to the consumer. For example, the more ice creams a child eats in an afternoon, the less will be the satisfaction derived from eating the next ice cream.

Economists tend to use not total utility as a measure of satisfaction, but marginal utility. Marginal utility may be defined as the amount of satisfaction to be derived from the possession of an extra unit of the good.

Utility is best described with the aid of an example. Consider the following.

A contractor has tendered for several jobs, requiring many loads of bricks. He decides that because there is a brick shortage that is expected to last for several months, he will buy up all the bricks he can. From the first load he buys he will derive a high satisfaction. The next load will give slightly less satisfaction and so on, as his worries, concerning the supply of bricks for the contracts, are reduced.

Finally the contractor may reach the point where he has no room left to stack any more bricks. At this point, the last load may have given him no extra satisfaction at all. (See Table 2.1.) There are no units of satisfaction, therefore notional units have to be allocated when considering utility.

Table 2.1 can be graphically represented as Fig. 2.1.

From the above, we can see that the more we have of a particular good, the less satisfaction we get from owning more of it. To show the effect of marginal utility in the above example, the number of loads of bricks can be plotted against the marginal utility, as in Fig. 2.2.

The effect of the law of diminishing marginal utility shows up clearly in

Table 2.1 Utility of loads of bricks

Loads of bricks	Total utility	Marginal utility
0	0	0
1	50	50
2	90	40
3	120	30
4	140	20
5	140	0

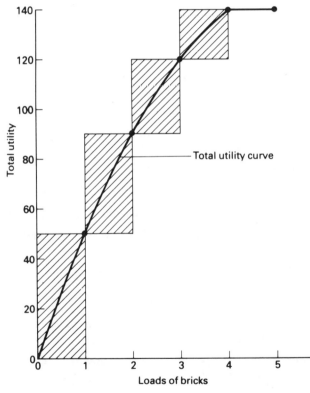

Fig. 2.1 Total utility

Fig. 2.2. This law states: the more a single commodity is consumed during any period of time, the less satisfaction will be given from the consumption of additional units of it.

This law of diminishing marginal utility applies to all goods in all situations with very few exceptions.

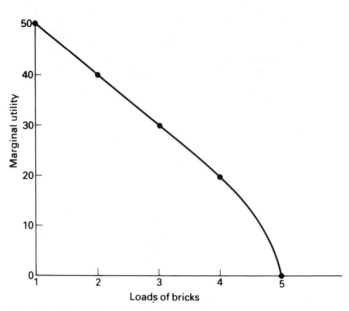

Fig. 2.2 Diminishing marginal utility

Economic problems of society

For any society, there are basically three economic problems to be resolved:

1. What commodities, and how much of each shall be produced?
2. How shall they be produced?
3. For whom shall they be produced?

Type and quantity of the various commodities

What and how much to produce is a very complex problem, and depends upon such points as:

(a) Are investment or consumption goods wanted? See Figs. 1.3 and 1.4. Can we do without consumption now, in order to improve production in the future?

(b) Is the society in question developed, or underdeveloped? Is it based on industry or agriculture?

(c) Is production for 'home' consumption, or are the goods to be exported?

(d) What input factors are available? This point is closely linked with point (b).

(e) What forms of goods should be produced? Should we produce arms for defence, or food for consumption in the home market? Food will satisfy individual wants. Defence will satisfy only a collective want of society.

(f) Is there competition from abroad?

(g) What government policies are likely to affect the production of the goods considered?

How are the goods to be produced?

Here again, many questions have to be answered before a final decision can be arrived at. Such questions might be:

(a) Are labour-intensive or capital-intensive methods to be employed? This point brings into focus many ideas raised earlier under labour inputs.

(b) What are the levels of unemployment in an area?

(c) Is it worth investing heavily in plant for the production process? This is governed by whether the demand is large and stable.

(d) Is it to be large or small-scale production?

(e) What types of resources other than labour are available?

(f) What government policies are likely to affect production methods? For instance, what form of energy should be chosen for furnaces, heating, etc.: should it be gas, electricity, oil or coal? We will see in later chapters that all forms of energy are affected by some form of government control.

For whom are the goods to be produced?

Before goods can be produced, there have to be customers who may be persuaded to buy them.

The type of customer often has an influence on production decisions, particularly with relation to the size of likely demand, and whether or not the demand is stable. Such questions relating to this problem may be:

(a) Is demand from within a country, or from other countries?

(b) How are export markets likely to be affected by government decisions?

(c) Are the goods to be produced for government, business enterprise or individuals?

(d) How are the goods to be distributed amongst the consumers?

Many of the above points will be discussed in later sections.

Entrepreneurs battle over such decisions daily, and these decisions may be reached on any of the three problems in different ways.

In certain industries, entrepreneurs may become so skilled in forecasting the likely demand for a particular good that they may take chances on decisions, being guided purely by instinct. The world of female fashions is based on the whims of fashionable ladies. No one knows for certain what style will be in or out of demand. Trends may suggest a certain direction, but no one is sure, and decisions on the styles to be produced often have to be based on intuition.

In most industries, however, a properly detailed marketing policy would help to answer many of the questions from the entrepreneur's viewpoint. (See Chapter 9.)

Types of economy

The three problems detailed above can all be affected by government action. In communist countries there is a great deal of State intervention in industry. There tends to be very little free enterprise, with most branches of industry being under State control. In such economies, a government can virtually dictate the type and quantity of goods to be produced, and also the methods of production to be used. The State also has a much greater say in who will consume the final goods.

An economy controlled purely by a central agency, with no free enterprise, would be a command economy. All decisions on allocation of resources etc. would be taken by this central agency.

An economy which is directly opposite in nature to the planned or command economy would be a free economy. A country operating a free economy would be following the *laissez-faire* policy of having no State interference in production or trading, and would allow the normal free enterprise system to work unhindered. Both free and command economies are extremes that do not usually exist in developed societies. (See Fig. 2.3.)

Most countries in the world today operate a mixed economy, that is, an economy that falls somewhere between the two extremes of planned and free economies. Britain today has a certain amount of government intervention in trade, which takes the form of taxes, control of interest rates, the issuing of grants and subsidies etc. One major area of government activity, however, is in international trade, as will be seen in later chapters. Trade in Britain still operates mainly along the lines of free enterprise, however.

It is doubtful whether a true free economy exists in a developed society, but it is in the context of just such a theoretical free economy that the **price mechanism** operates, to allocate the various resources available.

The price mechanism

In a free economy, there is by definition great freedom of choice. The owners of the factors of production are free to choose at what price and how much of their factors they will supply to production. The entrepreneur, on the other hand, is free to choose what type and quantity of factors are needed to supply goods at a certain price. Meanwhile the consumers decide what type and quantity of goods they want at the prices they can pay. Consumers, however, are also the owners of the factors of production, so the whole system tends to create a circular flow, as in Fig. 2.4.

Figure 2.4 can be divided into two interacting areas, the left side, which is concerned with the supply and demand of factors, and the right side, which is concerned with the supply and demand of produced goods.

Take for example a factory worker, who is an owner of the labour factor.

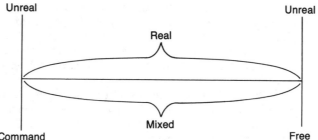

Fig. 2.3   Types of economy

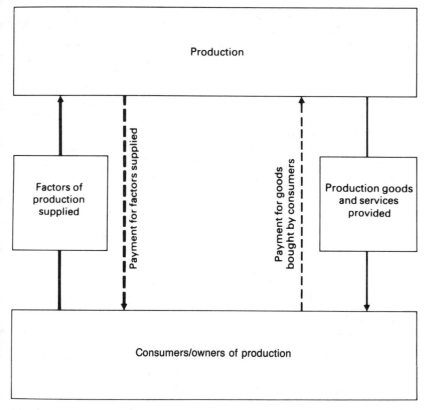

Fig. 2.4   The price mechanism in a free economy

He obviously wants the greatest reward he can obtain for supplying his labour, and so he finds a highly paid job. The high wages paid would also attract many other workers, and so, to attract just the right amount of labour, the entrepreneur may drop wages, as it would be wasteful to be paying too high a wage. If he does not drop wages, which would in practice be difficult to accomplish, he may decide to increase output. Society may buy the increased production, if it is wanted. If the increased supply of goods is not wanted, then the entrepreneur will cut back on production, and the workforce will have to find employment at other factories where goods are produced that are wanted by society.

To put this into the context of the construction industry, consider the following situation, simplified in Fig. 2.5. Assume in a small community, the only employers are a large brick-making company and a large joinery manufacturer. Over a period of several years demand for the two types of products has settled so that there is full employment, even with some overtime, and other resources supplied to the enterprises such as transport are fully utilised.

If there is now a relative change in demand for the two products, for example due to a change in consumer preference away from wooden windows and doors to PVC ones, the amount of wooden joinery leaving the factory will have to decrease. The entrepreneur may lay off staff, which may encourage workers to move to the brick-making factory, where perhaps overtime may be reduced so that more people could be employed. It may be possible to increase demand for joinery, by reducing prices, but in order to do this the fall in price must be reflected in the fall in wage rates. Labour would probably accept this if the alternative was unemployment.

If the opposite were to happen, where joinery manufacture suddenly increased, then more staff would be required. In this case higher wages might be offered to entice workers from the brick factory.

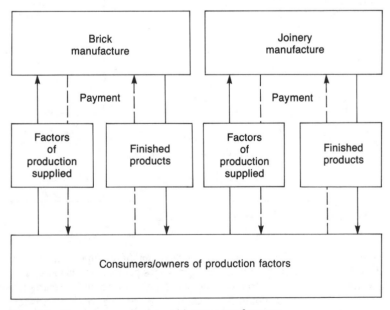

Fig. 2.5   The price mechanism with two manufacturers

Although this example is highly simplified, it shows how resources could be persuaded to move from one production unit to another by changes in society's demand.

It can be seen, then, that the price mechanism tends to allocate the factors to the areas where they are most wanted, and where they will give the most satisfaction to society.

The system tends to act as a delicate balance, weighing up the needs of society against the requirements of production. These needs, as was discussed earlier, are related to preference scales, and the marginal utility of the various goods.

In a real situation the mechanism would not operate quite so smoothly, due to the following:

(a) In a free economy, there would be no State involvement, therefore no State services such as defence or police would be available.
(b) Labour does not tend to move in search of work as easily as the system implies.

The real free economy does not exist in a developed society, and so in a mixed economy the operation of the price mechanism tends to work much slower than in theory, due to such factors as:

(a) Employers often keep on labour in the hope that sales will pick up, rather than pay out redundancy money.
(b) Workmen tend to stay in the working environment they know, with their friends, rather than move to a slightly better-paid job.
(c) Unemployed labour often stays where it is in the hope of eventually gaining employment. State-paid unemployment benefits often hinders mobility of labour.
(d) Production tends to be stockpiled, in the hope that demand for the product will rise. If demand does not increase, stocks will be cleared in sales.
(e) Government sometimes pays employers to keep people employed, rather than making them redundant.

Despite these various slowing factors, the price mechanism still works to a certain extent in a mixed economy.

In a planned economy the price mechanism would not be allowed to work, as all planning of resource allocation etc. would be undertaken by a central controlling agency, which might lead to greater efficiency in the long run.

The question must arise: what does society want? Does it want freedom of choice and a reasonably efficient economy. Or, does it want a dictatorial system where resources are allocated possibly more beneficially and goods distributed more fairly, but at the cost of society's freedom of choice.

Questions

1 Produce a scale of preference list, that government may draw up on behalf of the nation. (It will be interesting to compare your list with the discussion on government in later chapters.)

2 Discuss two situations where marginal utility might be a negative figure.

3 (a) A bottle of fresh water may have different utility to two different men travelling across the desert — why?

   (b) Discuss why a candle may have different utility to the same person in different situations.

4 Would a society based on a command economy, or a free economy, tend to have a better army?

5 Why are there so few true entrepreneurs today?

6 Explain, by the use of the price mechanism, how bricklayers might move from housing sites to sites where offices were being built.

Chapter 3

Cost—benefit analysis

Introduction

In the previous chapter, the allocation of resources was discussed. In a planned economy, decisions concerning problems of both industry and society are made purely by a central planning authority. In a mixed economy, however, government has to take a great deal more notice of what society wants. Decisions concerning commercial problems are settled by the entrepreneur using calculations on profitability as the main tool, with resources being allocated by the operation of the price mechanism. Where society is affected by far-reaching proposals, for example the siting of an airport, or the positioning of a new industrial estate, a means of scheme evaluation now gaining popularity is that of cost—benefit analysis.

Educated society of today insists that much more thought is given to all possible alternative schemes before arriving at the best solution obtainable. It is only by evaluating all alternatives that society in general can be best satisfied by choosing the proposal most suited to their needs.

In order to use cost—benefit analysis there should be alternative schemes to consider. They need not all be new schemes, for instance it may be possible to evaluate an existing shopping area, and compare it with an evaluation of the same area modified to allow the inclusion of offices and dwelling units.

Why is cost—benefit analysis needed? Surely the good old price mechanism can cope with all problems? It may be able to cope with the majority of situations where financial costs and returns are the only considerations, but what sort of society would it be, where everything was governed purely by profit?

Students may feel that society is concerned purely with profit. Certainly it plays a large part, but without safeguards of many sorts, how could society cope with the following?

(a) noise, dust and atmospheric pollution generally
(b) health
(c) ecological conservation
(d) parks and open spaces within urban areas

It is by constant vigilance by the public, and in particular certain pressure groups, that the environment in which we live is preserved.

Industry provides many benefits; it provides employment for workers, who spend their money within the local community, thus benefiting many others. Industry also benefits the community by satisfying their wants with the goods produced. However, it should be remembered that a benefit to one part of society need not necessarily be a benefit to all of society, indeed by giving to some sectors of the community, other sectors must often incur costs. A factory may provide employment, but this factory may also cause pollution, and a devaluing of local house prices, due to noise, increased road transport, etc. Cost−benefit analysis, then, is concerned with evaluating schemes for the whole of society, not just for isolated sectors, and for it to be valid it is essential to evaluate the effects on all affected parties. In an analysis studying two or three alternatives, the researchers may initially be looking for the scheme giving the best net gain to society in general. However, a particular scheme giving the highest net gain may not be the one chosen, as the sectors of society who gain, and those who lose, may not be distributed fairly. Consider the scheme shown in Table 3.1.

It is unlikely that society would allow scheme A to be adopted. Scheme B, although not quite so financially beneficial to society, is more evenly weighted to the affected sectors, and so is more likely to be carried out.

When carrying out evaluations, it may be that everyone is made better off by a particular scheme. Should this be the case, this is known as a pareto improvement as in scheme B.

In the majority of schemes, however, a potential pareto improvement is looked for. Here, certain sectors of the community benefit, and others lose. If the benefits are greater than the losses, then there is an overall social benefit, but not everyone gains personally.

Table 3.1

	Scheme A	Scheme B
Cost to wealthy	—	—
Benefit to wealthy	£1 m.	£0.4 m.
Cost to poor	£0.1 m.	—
Benefit to poor		£0.4 m.
Total benefit of	£0.9 m.	£0.8 m.

Potential pareto improvement can be converted into a pareto improvement if costless transfers of goods and/or money can take place among the various sectors of society. Transfer payments are those made other than in exchange for productive services. They may be gifts, but the most common form of transfer payments consists of those operated by government. Here payments are taken from certain sectors of the community in the form of income taxes etc., and are given to the poorer sectors in the form of grants, subsidies, income support payments etc.

It can be seen then that when first looking at scheme A, it seems very unfair. If transfer payments operate, the final outcome may be as follows:

original benefit to wealthy	£1 m.	transfer via taxes	− £0.5
original cost to poor	£0.1 m.	transfer via State aid	+ £0.5
final benefit to wealthy	£0.5 m.	} pareto improvement	
final benefit to poor	£0.4 m.		

By the operation of transfer payments, a grossly unfair situation becomes workable.

Method of carrying out cost—benefit analysis

Identification of the problem, and alternative solutions

This sometimes is more difficult than may first be imagined. It is necessary to evaluate not only any proposals put forward to date, including the existing scheme, but it may be necessary to question exactly what the objective is and whether there are any other methods by which that objective could be fulfilled.

Identification of the sectors affected

The extent of detail to which an analysis goes depends upon the problem and what one hopes to prove with the analysis. In theory whatever project is carried out, it could be argued that every person in the country is affected indirectly, e.g.

(a) Government taxes which are paid by the majority of people are needed to pay for roadworks, schools, reservoirs etc., therefore these projects are a cost to all people. Conversely they are also benefits to all people.
(b) Industrial pollution is not selective about whom it affects. Dust or noxious gases may give coughs or sore eyes to whole areas of population, depending upon the direction of the wind.

When carrying out cost—benefit analysis, it is better to concentrate on the sectors directly involved with the scheme. Remember, it is necessary to try and keep the evaluation as accurate as possible; the further the investigation delves into the fringe areas, the more inaccuracies are likely to be included.

Identification of the costs and benefits

The different sectors of the community may each have different types of costs or benefits allocated to them. Some benefits may be easily spotted, others may be much more difficult to determine. Two simple examples follow.

Example 1:   The building of a dam, and flooding of a Welsh valley to provide water for a Midlands town.

Benefits:
- To local residents, in the form of employment during construction of the dam.
- To the Midlands town, in the form of security of water supply.
- To sportsmen, in establishing a water-sports facility possibly with fishing.

Costs:
- The obvious loss of livelihood and heritage of the farmers, whose land is flooded.
- Possible ecological losses due to the flooding of swamps, in which rare birds nested, etc.
- Financial cost of the scheme.

Example 2:   The construction of a bypass road around a narrowly streeted village.

Benefits:
- Safer, less congested travel for road users.
- Less noise and smoke for residents of the village.
- Possible increase in house values in the village.
- Safety, health and welfare of shoppers increased.

Costs:
- Financial cost of the scheme.
- Possible loss of existing homes by people in the path of the new road.
- Noise and pollution transferred from village to outer housing areas.
- Reduction in house values close to the new road.

In order to aid researchers when carrying out an analysis, the public or other obviously affected sectors of society may be informed of the outline proposals and asked to comment. This may be done through local newspaper articles, prominently displayed notices in the location of the schemes or by surveys, either postal, telephone or personal. By informing society of outline proposals the response should help the researchers by indicating which groups feel stongly about the schemes and what it is that they are most concerned about.

The first example, that of flooding a valley, gives a good idea of one major difficulty in these evaluations. When do the costs and benefits accrue to the various sectors, and for how long do they operate? Employment would only be available to local labour while the dam was being constructed, so it is a very short-lived benefit. The provision of water for the Midlands may begin soon after the dam starts filling, and presumably will continue for many years. Fishing stocks may take many years to build up to a level that enables angling to be carried out.

Quantification of the costs and benefits

After identification of the relevant costs and benefits, the next stage is how to value them.

Financial costs or benefits are often fairly easy to calculate, but factors such as inflation, construction difficulties and possibly changing interest rates must also be considered. It has been said that if the final cost of the channel tunnel had been known at the outset, it would never have been considered. The correct costs and benefits must be used. For example, it may be stated that one benefit of a scheme is to reduce unemployment in an area. The benefit to the unemployed individual may be thought to be the value of the income he might now receive, but is it? Before gaining employment, the individual may have been receiving £120 per week unemployment benefit. If, when he obtains work, he now receives £180 per week, the benefit to him is £60 per week. Conversely if, as in Example 1 above, the bypass has reduced the value of a house from £160 000 to £149 000, the cost to the houseowner is £11 000.

The benefit of £60 and the cost of £11 000 are known as compensating variations and it is on such variations that evaluation should be based.

A compensating variation may be defined as the sum of money which, if received or paid after the scheme has been put into operation, would make the individual no better, or worse off, than before the change. It is then the opportunity cost, or opportunity benefit, of carrying out the scheme to the individual.

Government intervention in industry through subsidies, grants, taxes etc. makes it much more difficult to ascertain the true opportunity cost of factors or products. For example, a farmer may be encouraged to produce butter, and sell it cheaply, by giving him a government subsidy. If the cost of this butter entered into a cost—benefit analysis, it would be difficult to set a price on the butter, as the costs are not related to a free market situation in which the price mechanism sets prices. The butter cost included in an evaluation may be the shop price plus the subsidy paid to the farmer. This 'correcting' of prices to put them in line with the true opportunity cost of a free market situation is known as the setting of shadow prices.

The idea of shadow prices can be best demonstrated concerning a command economy. Imagine that a cost—benefit analysis is to be carried out concerning a production or service industry in such an economy. Because no free market situation exists to automatically set prices of factors and products, how can such an analysis be valued, as the prices charged for products or services may bear no resemblance to the true production costs? It is in such situations that prices will have to be 'corrected' to try to acquire a realistic figure.

With costs or benefits other than financial, these are often much more difficult to assess; indeed in some instances a quantitative analysis is impossible and a qualitative approach has to be adopted. Some examples of such problems are:

Example 3: A new road shortens the travelling time of 10 000 commuters, to and from their place of work. How is this measured? As travelling time to and from work is not generally carried out in the 'company's time' it would not be right to charge the time saved at the hourly work rate. So what rate

Table 3.2

	Time (hrs)	Cost (£)
By taxi	1	50
By train	$1\frac{1}{2}$	20
By bus	2	15

is chosen? It is necessary to try to determine a valuation of an individual's leisure time.

Consider the following, which may be one solution: The travelling habits of a large sample of a commuting community travelling a similar distance, are analysed as in Table 3.2.

A particular individual may decide to travel by train: thus, to save $\frac{1}{2}$ hour in leisure time, he pays an extra £5. From this it may be deduced that he values his leisure time at £10 per hour. Alternatively, an individual in a higher income bracket who may have very little leisure time, might travel by taxi. Here, he is willing to pay an additional £30 above the train fare to save $\frac{1}{2}$ hour. His leisure time is then valued at £60 per hour. Often, this degree of detail is not needed, and a time saving can be shown as a benefit by using the term $(t+)$ or $(t++)$. Conversely a time cost would be shown as $(t-)$ or $(t--)$ etc.

Example 4: The new road in Example 3 may create a great deal of localised traffic noise and pollution in the form of fumes, dust etc. How is this cost to the individual houseowner valued? One method often used, is to consider a similar scheme to that proposed, which has already been carried out in a similar environment. The effect on property values before and after the scheme is compared and this will give a ratio that can be applied to property values in the present scheme under consideration.

Example 5: This same new road may have to traverse a local beauty spot. How is the loss to the community of a pleasing natural landscape that is now spoilt to be valued? It is almost impossible to put a monetary value to this cost. It is most important, however, that such costs and/or benefits are included in a cost—benefit analysis, for the main reason for carrying out such evaluations is to take into account the effects on society in general. It was stated earlier that when a cost—benefit analysis is undertaken it must compare alternative schemes. If the alternative to the road cutting through the middle of the beauty spot is having the road skirt around the edge, then this second alternative is less of a cost when considering the landscape. It may be shown as an immeasurable or intangible cost by using a number of minus signs:

Road A (through beauty spot) $(i---)$

Road B (around beauty spot) $(i-)$

Should this appear in a table, it can be seen at once that road A has a higher social cost than road B. This, however, is about as much as can be deduced, if accuracy is to be maintained. With this last example it is always necessary to sample public opinion, to arrive at some measure of value, in the form of numbers of pluses or minuses.

Summary and conclusions

When carrying out an analysis, it may take dozens of people many months to complete, including many meetings with thousands of people. The results may run into hundreds or thousands of pages. One extreme example is of a report concerning the path of an oil pipeline across Alaska. The report took two years to complete and resulted in 4600 pages of script. It can be seen that it is essential to have the results summarised, so that the alternative schemes can be easily compared.

When the summary has been completed, conclusions can be drawn. The final decision may not always be the obvious one to the majority of people. When all the facts are presented, it is still often settled by taking notice of the groups with the loudest voices, or those with the greatest influence. During a cost−benefit analysis, and especially when decision time arrives, it is essential that the whole of society makes its views known, and helps to form a decision. If left purely to pressure groups, why bother with cost−benefit analysis?

An example of a simple analysis followed through

The problem

Many areas of North Wales suffer from traffic congestion during the peak holiday weeks during the summer. One such location is at Garth, as shown in Fig. 3.1. The road at Y leads to one coastal resort, whilst the road at X leads to another. The shortest route between X and Y at present is by following the path YSTX which goes over a toll bridge at A. As this bridge is only one lane wide and controlled by traffic lights, there is considerable congestion and delay at peak periods. The alternative route is by following the road YSWTX, involving an extra distance of 11 miles.

A further problem concerning the present situation is the weight restriction of two tons on the present toll bridge. All heavy traffic from factory F and the industrial estate plus other general heavy traffic has to take the longer route.

The proposals

One of the proposals, Scheme A, is to buy out the freeholder's interest in the tollbridge, demolish the existing bridge and construct a new two-lane bridge with pedestrian pavement, but at a lower level than the existing structure. Scheme B consists of putting another bridge across the estuary at B. This will be cheaper than scheme A, but will involve the demolition of two cottages.

Fig. 3.1 Garth

The sectors involved

(a) the local authority
(b) existing owners of the toll bridge
(c) residents of the village of Garth
(d) holidaymakers travelling by car
(e) businesses on the industrial estate and factory F
(f) yachting enthusiasts using the boat park BP
(g) owners of the demolished cottages at C
(h) a large heronry located at H by bridge B

The Costs and Benefits

(a) The local authority is involved with the financial costs of the alternatives, i.e. the direct costs of construction of schemes A or B. It could be argued that if the road system were improved it might help the letting of units on the industrial estate, which could be a financial benefit to the local authority, but this is more of an indirect factor and should not be considered.

(b) If scheme A went ahead the existing owners of the toll bridge would receive a lump-sum payment which in practice could be invested to provide an annual return. If scheme B went ahead the toll bridge would stay in position but the income from tolls would be reduced as more traffic would go via bridge B.

(c) The residents of the village of Garth would gain whichever scheme was adopted. If scheme A went ahead they could travel by car to X quicker. They could also walk across to the scenic pathway at T. At present there is no pedestrian traffic on the toll bridge. As there would probably be more traffic using the new bridge there would be a cost in the form of more pollution to those living at point P. If scheme B went ahead there would be a slight time saving in travelling to X during peak periods.

(d) Holidaymakers travelling by car from Y to X would save time in peak periods with both schemes.

(e) Both schemes A and B would show benefits to the businesses on the industrial estate and factory F in the form of time saving for heavy goods traffic.

(f) At the present time a dinghy sailing club uses a boat park shown as BP on the side of the estuary just inland of the existing toll bridge. The height of the existing bridgedeck allows the boats to pass underneath to enable them to race in the open sea. If scheme B went ahead this would not be affected, but if scheme A were adopted, the new bridge would be approximately 3 m lower, and so the majority of the boats would not be able to pass underneath. This would result in a new boat park having to be found on the seaward side of the new bridge.

(g) If scheme B went ahead two cottages at point C would have to be demolished. The owners, although compensated, would probably still lose out financially. There would also be costs in the form of upset and aggravation when moving house. If scheme A were adopted this sector would not be affected.

(h) At point H near the line of bridge B there is a heronry, reputed to be one of the biggest in the area. It is feared that if scheme B were constructed the traffic noise might disturb the birds, causing the nesting site to be abandoned.

Quantification of the Costs and benefits

(a) The local authority

The financial costs of the schemes are laid out in Table 3.3 and it can be seen that the financial costs of scheme A at £705 000 are more than twice those of scheme B at £330 000. If scheme A went ahead, and if the local authority could not obtain grants from central government for the works, the cost of the schemes would fall on local taxpayers.

(b) Existing owners of the toll bridge

At the present time the maintenance costs on the existing bridge are escalating. After taking into account running costs including staff salaries etc. and the actual income from tolls it is found that the net profit last year was £18 000. The purchase price of £250 000 if invested could return £20 000 p.a. If scheme A went ahead this would show a benefit of £2000 p.a.

It has been calculated that if scheme B went ahead a reduction in toll income would return a net profit of only £3000 p.a. Compared to the existing scheme (showing £18 000 profit) this would be a cost of £15 000 p.a.

(c) Residents of Garth village

If scheme A went ahead there would be a benefit in the form of being able to walk over the new bridge to the scenic walk. This could be shown as an intangible benefit $i+$. Residents at point P, however, might be subject to

Table 3.3 Financial considerations compared to existing

	Scheme A	Scheme B
Purchase of toll bridge freehold	250 000	—
Construction of bridge A	400 000	—
Associated roadworks to bridge A	55 000	—
Purchase of two cottages at C	—	80 000
Construction of bridge B	—	150 000
Associated roadworks to bridge B	—	100 000
Total capital costs	£705 000	£330 000

increased noise and dust pollution from increased traffic, and this could be shown as $i-$, an intangible cost. The advantage with scheme A would be the reduced aggravation of traffic queues and a time saving. In a real situation it might be possible to calculate a time saving and multiply it by the number of vehicle journeys; however, in this example it will be shown as $t+++$, a high time benefit.

If scheme B were adopted there would still be a slight time saving at certain periods of the year, but not as much as with scheme A because of the extra distance travelled. This could be shown as a low time benefit, $t+$. It must be remembered that we are considering travelling time throughout the year, not just at peak holiday periods.

(d) Holidaymakers travelling by car

As with the Garth residents both schemes show a time benefit over the existing situation. In peak holiday times, with the existing toll bridge, it sometimes takes 20 minutes to get from S to T. With scheme A it would take 3 minutes; it is therefore 7 times better or $t++++++$. To get from S to T with scheme B would take 10 minutes, or a time benefit of $t++$, as it is half the time.

(e) Businesses using heavy transport

For heavy transport to get from S to T it has to go via W, which takes 20 minutes. If the new times for schemes A and B were the same as for holidaymakers the time benefits would be the same, but all year round and not just at holiday periods.

(f) Users of the existing boat park

Scheme B would have no effect at all on the existing activities. Scheme A, however would result in an intangible cost in the form of upset and aggravation whilst a new site is found, and this could be shown as $i-$. There could be a financial cost if the club had to move to a new site, as the existing area is leased from a club member who farms on the estuary. This could be shown as $m-$, a monetary cost.

(g) Owners of demolished cottages

If scheme A went ahead this sector would not be affected. If scheme B were adopted the cottages would be demolished. The owners would receive compensation, but this seldom covers all costs involved, particularly with soft furnishings. There would therefore be a monetary cost or $M-$. There would also be the intangible cost $i-$ of moving house.

(h) The heronry

Scheme A would not affect the heronry, but if scheme B were constructed there would be a high intangible cost $i--$.

Conclusion

The student should bear in mind that this study is only intended to give an introduction to the methods used during cost—benefit analysis. This particular simplified example is only one way of carrying out an evaluation. Other people might have chosen slightly different affected sectors, and costs and benefits, but their final conclusions would probably have been the same.

In cost—benefit analysis, where a definite cost or benefit can be recognised, but where it is impossible to allocate a value in the form of an actual figure, the following abbreviations are often used.

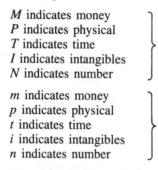

M indicates money
P indicates physical
T indicates time
I indicates intangibles
N indicates number

used where there is a once and for all, cost or benefit.

m indicates money
p indicates physical
t indicates time
i indicates intangibles
n indicates number

used where there is an annual flow of cost or benefit.

To determine whether each factor is a cost or benefit, a plus (+) or a minus (−) is put after the indicating letter. The greater the number of pluses, the greater the benefit. The greater the number of minuses, the greater the cost.

In a real situation, costs would have been investigated much more deeply, but it is doubtful whether it would have changed the order of preference for each sector. It is the final allocation of weightings to the various sectors that causes the most heated discussions in public debates, when conclusions are trying to be formed by the various parties concerned.

Table 3.4 Scheme A compared to the existing situation

	Costs	Benefits	Balance
(a) Local authority	705 000	—	− 705 000
(b) Toll bridge owner	—	2 000	2 000
(c) Residents of Garth	*i*−	*i*+ *t*+++	*t*+++
(d) Travelling holidaymakers	—	*t*+++++++	*t*+++++++
(e) Heavy traffic	—	*t*+++++++	*t*+++++++
(f) Yachtsmen	*I*− *m*−	—	*I*− *m*−
(g) Cottage C owners	—	—	—
(h) Heronry	—	—	—

Table 3.5 Scheme B compared to the existing situation

	Costs	Benefits	Balance
(a) Local authority	330 000	—	−330 000
(b) Toll bridge owner	15 000	—	−15 000
(c) Residents of Garth	—	t +	t +
(d) Travelling holidaymakers	—	t + +	t + +
(e) Heavy traffic	—	t + +	t + +
(f) Yachtsmen	—	—	—
(g) Cottage C owners	I− m−	—	I− M−
(h) Heronry	i− −	—	i− −

Table 3.6 Summary

	Scheme A	Scheme B	Order of preference A	Order of preference B
(a) Local authority	−£705 000	−£330 000	2	1
(b) Toll bridge owner	£2 000	−£15 000	1	2
(c) Residents of Garth	t + + +	t +	1	2
(d) Travelling holidaymakers	t + + + + + + +	t + +	1	2
(e) Heavy traffic	t + + + + + + +	t + +	1	2
(f) Yachtsmen	I− m−	—	2	1
(g) Cottage C owners	—	I− M−	1	2
(h) Heronry	—	i− −	1	2
Preference totals			10	14
Overall order of preference			1	2

On this basis scheme A would be chosen

Is it right to say that the travelling holidaymakers should have a larger weighting than the local authority or vice versa? Tables 3.4–3.6 show the summaries, which indicate that giving an equal weighting to all sectors would probably result in scheme A going ahead, as it has the lowest preference total in Table 3.6.

It may be felt that bigger weightings should be given to certain sectors; for example the financial cost is always a significant factor and could be weighted ×10 with the travelling holidaymakers and heavy traffic weighted ×2. Table 3.7 shows the resultant summary using a simple method of weighting, which would show a change in decision: scheme B would have been chosen as it has the lower total of 27.

38

Table 3.7 Summary with weightings

	Order of preference from Table 3.4		Weighting	Weighted order of preference	
	A	B		A	B
(a) Local authority	2	1	×10	20	10
(b) Toll bridge owner	1	2	×1	1	2
(c) Residents of Garth	1	2	×1	1	2
(d) Travelling holidaymakers	1	2	×2	2	4
(e) Heavy traffic	1	2	×2	2	4
(f) Yachtsmen	2	1	×1	2	1
(g) Cottage C owners	1	2	×1	1	2
(h) Heronry	1	2	×1	1	2
Preference Totals	10	14		30	27
Overall order of preference				2	1

With weightings shown as above scheme B would be chosen

Questions

For this exercise, students should work in twos or threes, in order that there should be some difference of opinion on values etc. This tends to give a more realistic impression of a practical situation.

The problem

The town of Hightown has for some years had a problem of increasing heavy traffic, going from a growing industrial complex north of the town down to the docks in the south. The main traffic flow travels along North Street (see Fig. 3.2) and has been causing many problems of noise, fumes, congestion and accidents. As a result of a fatal accident, greater pressure is being brought to bear on the authorities to construct a bypass around the town.

Scheme A (see Fig. 3.3) This proposes a bypass to the east and incorporates a new roundabout at point X, sweeping round and along the line of the existing Daniel Street, before continuing on to a new roundabout at point Y. It will be necessary to demolish 135 local authority dwellings and 30 shops on the east side of Daniel Street. A new flyover will also have to be constructed over Long Lane.

Scheme B (see Fig. 3.4) If carried out this will take the bypass to the west. It will again require a new roundabout at X, will sweep round to a new roundabout at Z on West Street, and on to roundabout Y. Due to a canal, it will be necessary to elevate a half kilometre section of roadway at point Q. This scheme will involve the demolition of 110 private dwellings.

Local authority housing

Shops and commercial properties

Private housing

Scale 2 cm = 1 km

Fig. 3.2 Hightown as existing

Prepare a cost–benefit analysis, comparing the two schemes with the existing situation. Remember, when deciding upon the weightings, if this method is used, that the schemes are proposed to improve the safety, health and well-being of the community of Hightown; financial cost may be of secondary importance.

40

Fig. 3.3 Hightown scheme A

Local authority housing

Shops and commercial properties

Private housing

Fig. 3.4 Hightown scheme B

Chapter 4

Economic growth

Introduction

What is meant by economic growth? Economists may talk of increases in gross domestic product (GDP), or of the increase in consumption per head, but both these indicators may imply one thing – the increase in the standard of living of the population as a whole.

It should be remembered that economic growth and increased living standards are not exactly synonymous. If one sector of society, say the entrepreneurs, increase their wealth, then there may be economic growth, but this does not necessarily ensure that the whole of society has a better standard of living.

How then can economic growth come about? If societies are studied from primitive to modern times, distinct stages can be seen along the way, which aid growth:

(a) Primitive self-contained villages eventually exchange goods, which tends to lead to specialisation.
(b) Exchange leads to better communication and transport systems.
(c) Exchange of goods also tends to lead to a system of barter and eventually necessitates a medium of exchange.
(d) Gradual growth of towns and population causes greater demand for goods.
(e) Further specialisation and division of labour sets the scene for mechanisation.
(f) Growth of industry.
(g) Large industrial production units seek more outlets abroad, to reap the benefits of large-scale production.

The development of society plays a large part in economic growth, but so also do other factors:

1. Capital investment. In Chapter 1, the argument was put forward of increasing capital investment at the expense of consumption goods. A country which has a relatively high standard of living and a well-developed industrial and commercial structure is better able to gear up for higher investment in capital than a less developed, mainly agrarian society. Unless aid is given to the less developed countries, the gap between the living standards of the two types of society will widen.

2. Country's population. Its age range, size and education plays a large part in determining the rate of economic growth, as discussed in Chapter 1.

3. Scientific and technical progress. This may bring about discoveries leading to new, more efficient manufacturing processes, innovations to machines or faster communication systems. The developments in micro-electronics in the late 1970s are even now continuing to revolutionise many aspects of society.

4. Demand for products. To establish an environment in which growth can take place, there should be a reasonable demand expected for the products produced. This demand needs to be at a high enough level to encourage entrepreneurs to invest in new capital equipment.

The fluctuations of the demand are often thought to be more important. A steady, relatively low demand may give more incentive for investment than a highly fluctuating demand with a higher average figure especially when large items of specialised plant are likely to be idle for long periods.

5. Division of labour. This results in greater efficiency within an enterprise, and may eventually lead to greater economic growth. Division of labour is the splitting up of a complex process into many simple stages. Thus instead of highly skilled craftsmen being required to produce a commodity, semi-skilled persons, who are nevertheless skilled in their own particular task, can produce the goods, often with the aid of machines which can carry out many of the simple but laborious actions.

Advantages of division of labour:

(a) It utilises a person's aptitude for a particular job, to the best advantage.
(b) It promotes skill and dexterity in performing a few simple tasks, thus giving a saving of time.
(c) It enables the increased use of machinery, which leads to standardisation and interchangeability of parts of the commodity being produced. The use of machinery also relieves the worker of laborious manual effort.
(d) There is more chance of finding a semi-skilled person to carry out the work, who will need the minimum of training for the job.
(e) As division of labour makes possible the use of machines, there is a stimulus for research to develop even better and faster production methods, which would be impossible under a system where division of labour did not operate.
(f) Higher wages are possible due to greater output.

Disadvantages of division of labour:

(a) Simplification of tasks tends to cause monotony.
(b) There is no possibility of the worker showing his artistic ability in the production of the article, as all products from the same production line will turn out the same. This leads to a decline in craftsmanship.
(c) There is a greater risk of unemployment, as there is more interdependence of workers on one another for a continuing operation. A disruption on one machine can stop a production line. Similarly in the car industry today, a disruption at a tyre-producing factory could prevent cars from leaving the car-production plant, which ultimately may lead to lay-offs at other component plants.
(d) With division of labour, there tends to be greater transportation of materials and components, whether it is within a factory, or whether the materials have to be transported from one plant to another.

In Britain the Industrial Revolution of the eighteenth and nineteenth centuries was the period in which division of labour flourished. It was of course carried out before that time, and has been since, but it was during that period that it had the greatest effect on the economic growth of this country.

6. Factors of production. The availability of the various factors of production obviously affects economic growth. In a labour-intensive economy, a lack of labour would obviously prevent growth, unless mechanisation could be introduced. The lack of money for investment in mechanisation or other large-scale schemes is a major problem in less developed countries. Expertise often has to be induced to come into the country to enable the development of new, or improvement of old, industries.

In the previous section, the various prerequisites and contributing factors concerning growth were listed. The student should constantly be trying to relate the points made earlier with the reality of British economic history, and, in particular during its heyday, the Industrial Revolution.

Brief economic history of Britain

The Roman occupation of Britain

The Roman invasion of Britain led by Julius Caesar began in 55 BC. The Romans were interested in Britain for two main reasons:

1. Its young men could serve in the Roman army.
2. The mining of minerals and the exploitation of other commodities such as wool, cloth and metalwork would be of great advantage to them.

At this time, there was specialisation taking place, people that worked in wood or metal, weavers of cloth, and potters. The various goods produced were exchanged within communities, or were transported by rough roads, or rivers, to ports, where trading was carried out with the Phoenicians and Greeks. Small coins were being used for currency, but much trade was carried out by exchange.

After the Roman invasion many new Roman towns were built, especially in the South. Forts, too, were built all over the country but more especially in the North and West, where the main opposition occurred to the occupation. Between the forts and towns were constructed the famous straight Roman roads, the major ones radiating from London, which even then was the main port in the country. The building of these roads greatly encouraged communication and road transport from one centre to the next.

The Romans also brought with them their own form of buildings, the best-known being the villa which was built to incorporate underfloor heating. The villa was a country home, which formed the centre of commerce for the district. The main occupation of these communities was based on the land, but the other needs of the people, in the form of pottery, weaving, woodwork and metalwork were also carried out at the villa. If coal or other minerals were available locally, mining would also be undertaken. Each of these communities was headed by a wealthy Roman, or in some cases a Briton who had slaves working for him. The villas operated a system of self-sufficiency, with most of their needs coming from within the community.

Overall, the Roman occupation of Britain caused the development of quite a sophisticated economic system with much of the trade of the urban centres depending upon the demand of the numerous officials and soldiers.

The period AD 410—1066

The last of the Romans left Britain in about 410 to defend their own country. This left Britain completely open to the attacks of the Saxons.

The Saxons had simpler tastes than the Romans, tending to settle in agricultural communities whilst totally ignoring the towns which developed under the Romans. With the disappearance of the demand for much of the commerce of the towns, the urban way of life had to be abandoned by many. In some areas, it is possible that a Saxon lord stepped into the shoes of a Roman, and took over the villa, running it on much the same lines as before. In general, however, the Saxons constructed dwellings and halls of a much less lavish nature.

It is thought probable that feudalism developed during this period. Feudalism was the system whereby each class was subservient to the one above. The system of agriculture was based on a three-field system, for example, one field grew oats, one barley and the other lay fallow. The next year the crops were rotated.

After the Saxon invasion and occupation, there were frequent attacks by the warlike Danes, who initially came to attack and plunder coastal villages rather than to find new areas for settlement. Eventually, however, the Danes did settle in Britain and this led to the splitting of the country into two, the North East under the Danish rule, and the South West under Saxon rule headed by King

Alfred. Alfred introduced various forms of taxation, as did the church, during this period. Alfred required the money to maintain defence and to placate the Danes by paying 'Danegold'. The Danish King Canute made laws, laying down the responsibilities and rights of each class of citizen. This helped to consolidate feudalism so that each person knew precisely his rights and position on the ladder of society. Towards the end of this period, towns were again growing in size and importance due to increasing trade and commerce.

The Middle Ages 1066—1300

William the Conqueror led the Norman invasion of Britain in 1066, and with it continued an era of expansion of the manorial system that had developed earlier.

The manor resembled, in some economic respects, the Roman villa, the manor itself being owned, or held on payment of allegiance to the king, by a lord, and occupied by dependent cultivators, the whole community being based on feudal lines.

The labouring class was granted the use of several strips of land by the lord, the payment for this being that the labourer worked so many days per week for the lord; the actual number of days depended upon the time of year and the manor to which they belonged.

Each manor sought to be self-sufficient, the main occupation still being based on agriculture, but most other requirements were also satisfied by specialists within the manor. Very few commodities had to be imported, only such things as metals, salt and tar, the latter being used to prevent sheep diseases. Due to the small-scale craft activities operating within the manors, there was little scope for manufacture or commercial activity outside that of normal village life.

Foreign trade was stimulated by the close relations between Britain and Normandy, and merchants and moneylenders started to arrive from overseas to encourage growth in commerce.

The crusaders also fostered trade with the East, and encouraged woollen cloth manufacture. The knights and lords who went to the Holy Land often found this exceedingly expensive, and many had to sell their lands to the newly emerging merchant class. This led to the undermining of the power of the barons, and proved to be the first step towards the decay of the feudal system.

Throughout this period Christianity flourished, and with it there was a strong feeling to despise wealth or extravagance. To many people, this acted as a deterrent to commencing any form of commercial activity that would have profited the individual. This outlook was one reason why foreigners were tempted to step in and carry out much of the trading at this time. Another reason for this Norman involvement was that they were much better organisers, in the governing of both commerce and the country.

Towns continued to grow throughout this period, although they were not very numerous, or very large. The Doomsday survey of 1086 recorded only 41 towns of any significance. London, of course, was the trading centre of the nation, and as such was the largest urban area. Towards the end of the Middle Ages, many towns were able to buy the right of self-government from the lords who originally owned the land; this was known as the purchasing of a charter. The towns then had the privilege of levying local taxes, the power to conduct their own courts, and often the power to hold local markets. These markets or fairs were generally held weekly, and were of considerable importance, as this was where the majority of trading took place.

The period 1300—1750

The operation of the manorial system began slowly to break down during this period.

The lowest working class, the serfs, objected to having to work for the lord, and consequently the lords found it was more beneficial to both sides to pay wages for work caried out by the serfs. The serfs in return paid rent for their land holdings.

The unplanned growth of towns often resulted in many epidemics of plague and typhoid, due to the filth and rubbish left in the streets, which often polluted the water supply. Remember, at this time, there were only wells for water and the effluent from crude toilets sometimes seeped into these water supplies. The worst of these plagues was the Black Death, which occurred in 1348—49. It effectively halved the population of Britain, and made the old manorial system very difficult to manage, due to the competition for the available labour. Because of the limited labour supply, wage rates rose, and this resulted in the *Statute of Labourers* being passed in 1351. This tried to limit the wages to the old rates, but was very unpopular, and was in many instances ignored. General unrest amongst the working classes resulted in 1381 in the 'peasants' revolt', led by Jack Straw and Wat Tyler. The revolt did not accomplish a great deal, as the lords were determined to try to maintain the status quo, to enable manor life to continue as before. Eventually, however, changes did occur, and many lords let out their lands, freeing serfs who were still operating the old system.

In the manorial system, the available land was of four types:

(a) that owned and used by the lord, but worked by serfs
(b) that used by serfs
(c) common land, on which the serfs had the right to graze cattle
(d) waste land, from which firewood was collected by all

With the difficulty concerning labour, much of the agricultural land which initially consisted of many strips, was converted into large fields, and vast areas of common land were also 'enclosed' to graze sheep on. Sheep rearing was far less labour intensive, and also there was a great demand for wool, both for export, and for the manufacture of cloth, which was often carried out in village cottages.

In the sixteenth century, Henry VIII destroyed many monasteries, and their lands and buildings were often used in the woollen industry.

The decline of the manorial system tended to create a drift of population from the country to the towns. With the increase in sheep farming, the land was not now available for the serfs to work, neither were their services required.

In the towns, many found work in the developing crafts and industries. Many, however, did not, and these added to the ranks of the many paupers already existing in urban life.

During the seventeenth century, there was a considerable growth in industry, which has become known as the Minor Industrial Revolution. Coal mining was one of the first forms of large-scale capital enterprise, needing many people to put up money to enable funds to be available for the sinking of shafts. With deep-shaft mining, it was many months from the sinking of the shafts to the actual mining of the coal, hence the need for large sums over long periods. Iron-ore mining and foreign trade were also financed by a joint stock method. As early as the sixteenth century, the merchant adventurers had established trading links in the far corners of the world, and this resulted in trading companies being set up:

Muscovy Company in	1555
Levant Company in	1581
East India Company in	1600
Hudson's Bay Company in	1670

The Agrarian Revolution

During the seventeenth century, many improvements were made to agricultural methods. Much of the unused wasteland was being converted to agricultural land, by clearing woodlands or draining marshes and fens.

Another great advance was a change in the method of farming the available land. The open field system, which was the one used by the manorial system, was wasteful in time and effort, as it necessitated the working of scattered strips of land. It was also wasteful as one field was always left fallow. By enclosure, and by rotating certain crops, greater returns could be obtained from the land.

It was Lord Townshend who first used the root crops of turnip, mangel-wurzel or swede in rotation with grain or clover crops.

Up to this time, many beasts had to be killed off in the autumn as there was very little winter fodder to keep them through the winter. Turnips proved to be an ideal cattle food, and helped keep large stocks of cattle for breeding the following year.

In 1701, Jethro Tull invented a seed drill, which improved enormously the return obtained over broadcast sowing. Horses proved to be 50 per cent faster than oxen, which was the traditional motive power, and in 1714 Tull invented a horse-drawn hoe.

During the seventeenth and eighteenth centuries, scientific breeding and cultivation methods started to result in better strains of animals and crops, which enabled higher yields to be obtained.

With these various improvements, there was now a better chance of feeding the growing population of urban dwellers, who could no longer grow their own food.

The Industrial Revolution

This is generally understood to cover the period from about 1760 to 1850. During this time there was considerable economic growth, which affected not only industry, but social and political life as well.

No single factor was responsible for the Industrial Revolution, but more likely it was due to the culmination of many developments which arose in previous centuries. Such factors might include:

(a) politically strong and united, with no internal strife at this time
(b) merchant contacts in many parts of the world, ensuring an expanding export market
(c) climate suitable for processing wool and cotton, which were the main exports
(d) banking and credit facilities well developed
(e) large resources of iron and coal ready for exploitation, in close proximity to one another
(f) capital had been built up by foreign trade

At this time, there was considerable profit to be made in the trading of cotton and slaves, between Britain, West Africa and America. Britain also imported many raw materials, and re-exported finished goods, particularly textiles and metalwork.

There was a great deal of discontent among the working classes for many had been forced into the town by enclosure, and entrepreneurs, quick to realise that labour was plentiful, succeeded in suppressing wages for many years. The workers had to live in tiny slums, and were often forced to buy from company shops on credit, and so they never effectively got out of debt. The labourers had very few rights, and working conditions were harsh. Children were often sent out to work at the age of five, to oil unguarded machinery in the factories, or to carry out other simple tasks. In many factories, the workers were fined for petty offences, whilst having to work long hours for poor pay. The lack of a piped water supply and proper drainage still caused much disease in the overcrowded towns. It is not surprising that the working class got very frustrated with its situation, but could do very little, as the entrepreneurs were well represented in parliament, whereas the workers were not.

The first population census was not carried out until 1801; figures up to that date are therefore based on estimates (Table 4.1). In the centuries preceding 1700, the population is thought to be fairly static, perhaps growing only slightly. So why in the eighteenth century does the population suddenly start to increase so fast? Several reasons have been put forward for this:

(a) There may have been an increasing birth rate, but more importantly, there was thought to be a marked decline in the death rate.
(b) The improvements in agriculture were producing more food, which led to less starvation and better diets.
(c) Many workers were no longer tied to craft apprenticeships which meant that they were free to marry earlier in life.

Table 4.1 Population of England and Wales

Date	Total (m.)	Percentage increase on previous figure
1700	$5\frac{1}{2}$ estimated	—
1750	$6\frac{1}{2}$ estimated	18
1801	9 census	39
1851	18 census	100
1901	33 census	83
1951	44 census	33
1990	51 census	25
2031	55 projected	7

Source: Annual Abstract of Statistics

(d) Interest in medicine and hygiene started to develop.
(e) Large families produced a greater income, as the children often worked from an early age.

Whatever the reasons for its growth, the larger population added fuel to an increasing consumer demand, giving industry greater incentive to increase output.

Technical and scientific growth

Since the time man first started to use tools, innovation and discovery have led to improvements in his standard of living. Through the centuries, this improvement was initially very slow, but with better communications, and greater demands from both manufacturers and agriculture, invention continued, and still does so today, at an almost exponential rate.

Below are listed just a few of the important discoveries concerning industry. Remember, however, that the advances made in agriculture are just as important to the growth of this era.

(a) In 1733 John Kay invented the flying shuttle, which greatly increased both the speed of weaving and the width of cloth that could be produced.
(b) James Hargreaves produced in 1767 the first successful spinning machine, the spinning jenny. This invention is often thought by many to mark the beginning of the Industrial Revolution.
(c) Coal mines during the late seventeenth century were getting deeper, due to the surface deposits having been worked out. Deeper shafts encountered problems of flooding, but this was overcome, for in 1705 Newcomen patented a steam pump for pumping out shafts.
(d) Several people tried to improve on the steam pump, without great success, but in 1781, Boulton and Watt developed a viable steam engine. Their

factory turned out many of these engines, for use in mills, potteries and breweries.

(e) One problem when the steam engine was first developed was that of accurately boring the cylinders. Jack Wilkinson of Broseley overcame this problem, making the steam engine a great deal more reliable and durable.

(f) In the 1790s, Joseph Bramah invented a wheel cutting machine, a machine for making locks, and also the hydraulic press. At this time, a colleague of Bramah, Henry Maudsley, devised a screw cutting lathe.

The Industrial Revolution gave great encouragement and impetus to engineers and inventors, as the faster scientific discoveries were made, so technologists had to devise practical ways of making the discovery usable in industry.

From the early 1800s the growth of many large industries has continued, and these were often based on simple discoveries or inventions.

(a) From the 1830s the railway industries grew.

(b) Shipbuilding started to grow during the 1850s.

(c) The start of the motor car industry was in the 1890s.

(d) Aircraft and radio engineering grew from 1900.

(e) From the 1940s grew the electronics and nuclear industries.

Development in transport

Roads

Up to the end of the seventeenth century, much transport was carried out by coastal and river vessels, due to the fact that roads were very poorly developed, and ill maintained since the Romans left.

There was considerable pressure to improve transport and communication facilities, for military reasons and to enable goods from industry and agriculture to be more widely distributed.

Between 1750 and 1800 there were many turnpike roads. People were granted the right to charge a toll for the use of the road, in exchange for maintaining it. These gradually disappeared towards the end of the nineteenth century due mainly to competition from the railways. The last tolls were abolished in 1895, the responsibility being transferred to Highway District Boards. In 1909 the Road Improvement Board was formed to administer the funds raised solely for roads by the imposition of a road-fund tax. As roads developed it became obvious that a national plan for road transport was needed. This led eventually to the construction of the motorway systems of the 1960s and 1970s.

Canals

Due to the rapid growth in the mid-eighteenth century, great demands were placed on the poor transport facilities available.

In 1761 the first canal, the Bridgewater canal, was constructed to link Manchester with a colliery at Worsley. This proved a great success, and was extended from Manchester to Runcorn. Following this, other canals were constructed, the Trent and Mersey in 1777, the Leeds and Liverpool in 1777 and many others, until construction peaked in about 1792. Finance for their construction tended to dry up, but they still managed to find backers and continue building into the nineteenth century.

The development of the railways in the 1830s marked the start of the decline of the canals.

Initially, canals were financed and owned privately, like the turnpike roads. The Transport Act of 1947, however, brought the majority of inland waterways into public ownership. For several decades after this, the canals' traffic continued to decline, until a recent interest for leisure activities caused a revival in the 1960s.

Railways

Railways, or as they were known initially, plateways, had existed at coal mines from the seventeenth century. Plateways were similar to railways, except that the rails were of wood, and the motive power was horses or men. Various experiments were tried with steam power, but it was not really until 1825 when George Stephenson improved his locomotive design and the Stockton and Darlington railway was opened, that the era really began.

In 1830 the Liverpool to Manchester railway was opened, and the Rocket started its service.

The heyday for railway construction was 1830–50, and by the end of 1850, 9600 km (6000 miles) of track had been constructed.

The railways had many advantages for society:

(a) Cheap rapid transport for people and freight to many parts of the country.
(b) Faster communication, particularly for newspapers and mail.
(c) It encouraged time to be standardised at Greenwich mean time. Up until 1852, when the telegraph lines were completed, it was impossible to verify time accurately in different parts of the country.

Railways again, like the early roads and canals, were privately financed and in the early days large fortunes were made or lost on transactions involving railway companies. Track continued to be laid up until 1900, and by 1914 there were 32 000 km (20 000 miles) of track.

Since then there has been a steady decline in the length of track in use, due mainly to increased motor transport.

From 1830 onwards the railways have been subjected to a great deal of legislation covering many aspects, under such topics as safety, maximum fares, accounting methods, and hours and wages of employees.

The Railways Act of 1921 led to the amalgamation of 121 separate railway companies into four. The London, Midland and Scottish Railway; the Great Western Railway; the London and North Eastern Railway; and the Southern Railway; it was hoped that this would bring economies, and lead to a better, cheaper service for the customers. The railways, however, still continued to lose money, due not only to competition from road transport, but also because of labour troubles, and a general decline in trade particularly between 1914 and 1939. Until 1939, the railway companies had to apply to the Railway Rates Tribunal before any increase in fares was allowed. In 1939 the Transport Advisory Council suggested that the companies should be allowed to charge whatever fares they thought fit. The government took over the organisation of the railways in 1939 with the outbreak of war. After the war, the great deterioration that had taken place had made it almost inevitable that nationalisation in some form would occur. This happened with the advent of the 1947 Transport Act. As a result, on 1 January 1948, the four main railway companies were taken over by the British Transport Commission. At the same time, the commission also obtained control of harbours, inland waterways and road haulage. From 1948 to the present day, there has been massive investment in the railways. Even so, today they have great problems in breaking even, despite the cutting of uneconomical rural services, and further mechanisation. In the 1970s, the track being used measured about 18 000 km (11 000 miles) compared with 32 000 km (20 000 miles) in 1914. Staff in the 1970s numbered about 250 000 against 700 000 in 1948.

Perhaps with problems of road congestion and the soaring cost of oil, the economics of rail transport may cause it once again to be the main means of transport in the years ahead.

Social problems and attitudes throughout the ages

In the sixteenth century, pauperism rose to such proportions that in 1601 a poor law was passed, putting the parish in charge of administering relief to this ever-growing sector of the community. This relief was financed by the levying of a poor rate on households.

In 1722 the Workhouse Act was passed, and under it, unemployed people were required to work at these houses which were often contracted out to industrialists. If the unemployed refused to work, then they received no benefit. The object of this Act was to relieve the householders of the burden of the poor tax. In practice it did not have much effect on the level of tax, as pauperism still continued to increase. In the 1790s under threat of possible revolution, the Speenhamland system developed. This consisted of parishes supplementing low wages, thus preventing starvation conditions. The amount paid was related to the price of bread, and the size of a person's family. The result of this was that employers tended to keep wages low, knowing that the workers would receive a supplement. Again this threw a heavy burden on the poor rate.

At the beginning of the nineteenth century there was a change of direction concerning social ideas. There were three main reasons for this:

(a) T. R. Malthus published his various essays on population, which attracted a large following. Basically his theory was that unless parents decided voluntarily to restrict the size of family, then population would continue to rise, which would result in no increase in the standard of living.

(b) There was in 1830 a labourers' revolt mainly in areas where existing supplementary payments were highest. This indicated the necessity of reform.

(c) The ever-increasing burden of the poor rate on the rest of society.

The Poor Law Amendment Act of 1834 was the result. It tended to cut relief to a minimum, thus making it more financially beneficial for people to seek employment, rather than rely on supplements. In general it aimed at making workers, rather than the parishes, responsible for supporting themselves and their families.

Throughout the nineteenth century, following this attitude of *laissez-faire*, there was considerable economic growth. The wealth, however, was by no means equally distributed, with the entrepreneurs becoming richer to the cost of the workers. One major problem was that most workers were employed as casual labour, and due to political problems in the overseas markets, they often found themselves out of work. In 1909 the first Labour Exchanges were set up, their name being changed in 1916 to Employment Exchanges, when the Ministry of Labour was formed. Following Lloyd George's National Insurance Act of 1911, National Insurance Benefit was paid within selected industries, and the Old Age Pension Act of 1908 had provided a pension to all over the age of 70, subject to certain conditions.

The depression of the inter-war years led to further benefits (dole money) being paid in addition to the minimal poor-law relief which still continued to be administered by poor-law unions.

In 1934 the Unemployment Assistance Board took over the relief of all those who were now entitled to benefit; also the administration of the poor law was put in the hands of a national agency.

In the 1930s and early 1940s, there was much pressure for reform, which resulted in the *Beveridge Report* of 1942. These proposals outlined State involvement to give aid 'from cradle to grave', and included unemployment benefits and measures for re-employment, besides a health service and family allowance.

During 1945–46, the Labour government embodied these ideas into several acts:

(a) The Family Allowance Act of 1945, where allowance would be paid from general taxation revenue.
(b) The National Health Service Act 1946 which gave care to all, financed from the National Insurance fund, rates, and from taxation.
(c) The National Insurance Act 1946 set out payments for sickness, retirement, unemployment, maternity, family allowances and death. These were paid for out of funds collected from employer, employee and the State.
(d) The National Assistance Act of 1948 led to the formation of the National Assistance Board to administer benefits along the lines of the old poor law, to anyone whose needs were not met by the previous Acts of 1945 and 1946.

It was hoped that these supplements would ease as wages increased. Many people, however, still experienced hardship, and this continues even today.

Since the 1934 Special Areas Act, government has tried to relieve unemployment in areas of declining industry, by grants and loans to new industries, in an attempt to create employment. Other Acts followed in 1936 and 1937 and some areas which were particularly depressed were designated Special Areas. These included south Wales, much of the north-east, and the central lowlands of Scotland.

In 1945 the Distribution of Industry Act renamed the Special Areas as Development Areas, and in 1947 it became necessary to obtain an industrial development certificate (IDC), before a factory could be constructed above a certain size. By using the granting of these IDCs as an incentive, much industry was persuaded to move into development areas.

In 1960 the method of designation was changed, the Development Areas being replaced with Development Districts, and defined as any Employment Exchange District where unemployment was over $4\frac{1}{2}$ per cent.

The 1966 Industrial Development Act replaced Development Districts by the present Development Areas. These now include larger areas than previously, and include the whole of northern England, the majority of Scotland, and most of Wales, Cornwall and North Devon.

In the 1970s the government granted much money to many industries in an attempt to preserve or create jobs. Many other measures, besides grants, were carried out in the late 1970s, including:

(a) From 1977 firms in Special Development Areas with fewer than 50 employees received £20 per week subsidy for each additional worker employed.
(b) Various other payments and subsidies which tended to aid new employment possibilities, especially for school leavers and people needing retraining.

With Britain's entry into the EC there is a common policy to improve employment opportunities by increasing the mobility of labour. The following actions were taken by the Council of Ministers in 1974:

(a) Equal pay for men and women.
(b) Standard 40-hour week, and four weeks annual holiday.
(c) Procedures were suggested for mass dismissal and for the rights of workers when transferred between different firms.

See also Chapter 18.

The development of banking

During the Middle Ages, it was thought wrong, both by the Church and by the State, to charge interest for the loan of money. This view, not unnaturally, led to most people having to finance their commercial activities from their own funds, or with the help of friends and relatives. With the developing of industry and commerce there was a change of mood, which eventually led to Acts during the late sixteenth and early seventeenth centuries legalising the charging of interest. The way was now clear for the commencement of the modern banking system.

It spite of the feelings of society, money lending had taken place from early times. During the early fourteenth century the Lombards, who were wealthy

Italian merchants, settled in London and were granted an area of land which became known as Lombard Street. They carried on trading mainly as goldsmiths, but also as pawnbrokers and bankers. As finance for trading became necessary banking activities expanded considerably, although throughout the seventeenth century it was carried out side by side with pawnbroking and goldsmithing.

At the end of the seventeenth century the receipts that private bankers gave to their customers for the deposit of bullion came to be widely accepted as currency, and a banker by the name of Francis Childs was reputed to be the first to produce printed banknotes. Many banks followed Childs' example, and printed their own notes.

With the increasing expansion of trade, the small private banks found it difficult to cope with the large-scale activities which were now requiring finance. The Bank of England resulted, and was founded by Royal Charter in 1694, its capital coming from public subscription.

The activities of the Bank of England at this time consisted of:

(a) Accepting deposits and making loans.
(b) The issue of banknotes. Between 1708 and 1826 it had the monopoly of banknote issue, in banks with over six partners.
(c) Discounting bills of exchange.

The Bank initially made a loan to government of £1 200 000, which was another major reason for the allowing of its formation. From the outset, the bank maintained very close links with the government, and in 1751 it took over the majority of the national debt. Further loans were made to government from time to time, and eventually it was thought necessary in the nation's interest to nationalise the Bank in 1946.

The Bank of England certainly helped trade in London, it also helped government, it did not, however, solve the need for large-scale banking in the provinces. The Bank had no intention of setting up branch offices, until it was threatened in the 1820s by bankers wishing to set up joint-stock banks.

The smaller private banks, i.e. those controlled and financed by one owner, had to cater for these areas, particularly up until 1826 when the Bank of England's note issue monopoly was lifted in all areas except London. Before 1826 the private banks experienced two main problems:

(a) lack of capital
(b) frequent runs on the banks, which led to a general lack of confidence in small banks

The obvious answer was to have joint-stock banks, i.e. those controlled and financed by several people, as the facility then existed for obtaining more capital should it be required. After 1826, joint-stock banks were allowed to issue notes, which was regarded as an essential part of banking, and after this date joint-stock banking increased.

In the 1830s and 1840s these newly formed joint-stock banks had to struggle for survival as they were often suppressed by legislation. The Companies Act of 1862 detailed the law with regard to joint-stock banks, and classed them the same as other forms of trading companies, particularly with regard to limited liability. It should be noted that other forms of trading had enjoyed limited liability since 1855. The 1862 Act gave security to the banks. During the next 130 years, mergers took place which eventually reduced the number to six main banks: Barclays, Coutts, Lloyds, Midland, Natwest, and Williams and Glyn's.

Gilds

During the Middle Ages, trade between towns and within individual towns were carried out by merchants. For mutual protection these merchants started to form their own associations or gilds. Eventually the gild merchants had monopoly of trade within their own town, and outsiders were only permitted to trade with members of the gild.

The gilds not only protected the merchants, but also the townspeople, as the gilds fixed fair prices, and checked weights and measures. They were administered by a council with an alderman at the head. There were also wardens whose duty it was to enforce the rules, and offenders would suffer fines, or expulsion from the gild.

The welfare of its members was another activity undertaken, as the gild looked after the sick, and the widows and children of its members.

From the twelfth century, groups of craftsmen also formed gilds, often for maintaining good standards and self-protection. In many instances the merchant gilds insisted on craft gilds being formed, to enable better control of that particular activity. These craft gilds were separated by craft, so that many could exist in one town. This was unlike merchant gilds, where only one generally existed in a particular town. They were organised along similar lines to the merchant's, with standards being assured by the use of warders.

Within the craft gilds were three levels of workman − the mastercraftsman, the journeyman and the apprentice. Initially, many boys were taken on as apprentices, who were bound to their master for the duration of the apprenticeship, usually seven years.

Journeymen were those who had completed their apprenticeship and who worked for the master for wages. The journeyman was considered the halfway stage between apprentice and master, and he could in theory leave the master at any time, to set up his own workshop. In practice this often had to be sanctioned by the gild. As gilds developed they became more exclusive, and eventually only the sons of craftsmen were taken on as apprentices, and even then a premium had to be paid.

The mastercraftsmen were the owners of the business, and it was these people who were responsible for ensuring that apprentices were properly trained and that standards were obeyed in each business.

Like the merchant gilds, there existed a welfare system, and some gilds ran their own schools. Religion played a large part in their activities, and each mystery or craft often performed mystery plays. These were plays portraying a scene from the Bible concerning the particular craft in question.

In the fourteenth century, as the craft gilds became stronger, the merchant gilds found that they could no longer supervise the various trades, and consequently lost much of their powers with regard to the crafts.

As trade expanded, the mastercraftsmen developed further their role as employers of labour, and so prospered, and evolved into a middle-class society which laid the foundation of Britain's expanding trade in the centuries to come. The journeymen at this time became aware that there was little chance of ever becoming masters, and in order to divorce themselves from the same controlling gild as the masters, they set up journeymen associations, or yeomen's gilds. It has been argued that these were the earliest form of trade union, as they were trying to secure reasonable working conditions, hours of work and wages for the working classes.

As industry developed still further in larger workshops, and ultimately into factory systems, the craft gilds found that they no longer had a monopoly hold over the supply of a specialised craft labour. Due to the division of labour it was not often required by the new production methods. The gilds also had no hold over the quantity or quality of products being produced, and there followed a gradual decline in the craft gilds. The yeomen's gild did not last long, due to lack of finance, and the fact that they constantly had to battle against very influential people.

Trade unionism

In the Middle Ages, craft gilds contained both the masters and the workers, both often living in the same house, and together they worked in a harmonious atmosphere. As society developed more and more the idea of profit-making, there came a rift between the employers and the employees which continues to grow ever wider to this day, according to some points of view. The Industrial Revolution saw employers fighting, with the aid of parliament, to quell the demonstrations of the overworked, underpaid workers.

Until the Industrial Revolution, much work was done on a domestic level, particularly in the woollen industry. Here middlemen would take raw wool to the peasants' cottages for the family to turn into cloth. The worker in this environment could, to a large extent, please himself how hard, and what hours, he worked. With the advent of larger, powered machinery, it was often only financially feasible to set up the large-scale production in factories. These new factories could be managed more efficiently than the old outworker system, and soon undercut the price of domestically produced products. This inevitably drew many workers to the new factories. These workers had to adjust to much more discipline, working set hours for low wages in conditions they could not improve themselves. Add to this the squalor that many townsfolk had to live in, and one can start to understand the environment in which worker unrest flourished. Workers began to combine together to try to improve wages, but when this came to the ears of government there was grave concern. It was felt that any type of reform might lead to revolution, as had just taken place in France in 1789. The result was the passing of several Acts from 1796 to 1801, all of which were generally referred to as the Combination Acts. These prevented the combination of workers, for the purpose of trying to raise wages.

The arguments put forward against combination were:

(a) This tended to restrain trade.
(b) Should higher wages be paid, British goods could no longer match up to the competition of cheaper foreign goods in our overseas markets.

These Acts stayed in force until they were repealed in 1824, thanks to the efforts of Francis Place. After 1824, many trade unions flourished, but after the middle of the century, violence erupted again which resulted in the passing of the Trade Union Acts of 1871, 1875, and 1876. These clarified precisely the legal position of the unions, giving them the right of peaceful picketing, without the participating members being accused of conspiracy.

Throughout the 1830s and 1840s, workers tried to strengthen their position by forming first national unions of particular trades, and eventually general unions which were composed of all trades. During this period, Robert Owen with his ideals of co-operative ownership founded the Grand National Consolidated Trade Union (GNCTU) in 1834. The union was formed by the amalgamation of several large trade unions, the idea being that a single large national union could wield a 'bigger stick' than several smaller unions. However, instead of unified action, the individual unions tended to look after their own members, rather than the wider aspects of the national union. This resulted in many small local disputes, which destroyed the GNCTU before national strikes could be arranged.

In 1851 the 'new model' trade union came into being with the Amalgamated Society of Engineers (ASE). This union had a centralised expert administration and a back-up of large funds, most of which were used for welfare in the form of sick pay, unemployment pay, and pensions. There was still the possibility of strikes, but peaceful picketing and negotiation was generally preferred. Other unions followed the example of the ASE, and it was largely their efforts that brought about the legislation of 1871–75. One of the major union successes of this period was in 1889 when the London dockers won their 'dockers' tanner' per hour.

By the close of the century, many unions and employers had agreed on negotiating and grievance procedure, and many wages boards and committees were in existence.

In the 1890s workers were content to have orderly pay negotiations, but by 1910 their attitudes had changed. In 1906 the Labour Party was formed, and by 1908 there were 50 Members of Parliament sympathetic to the workers' problems. Union membership at this time was $2\frac{1}{2}$ million, which rose to $4\frac{1}{2}$ million by 1914. In 1919 unions again grew militant and in 1926 much disagreement, particularly in the mining industry, resulted in the general strike of 1926. It lasted only 9 days before the men reluctantly returned to work.

In the 1930s and 1940s membership continued to grow, and began to encompass clerical and professional workers in addition to the trades already catered for. In the early 1980s membership had grown to about 12 million but today the figure has dropped to around 7 million. During the 1960s and 1970s the unions developed into an extremely strong negotiating force. It was viewed by government as a potentially damaging situation, as ever-increasing union demands for increased wages could have jeopardised the United Kingdom's competitiveness in world trade. For this reason the Conservative government during the 1980s deprived the unions of some of their power, in particular tightening up on picketing. Today unions still exist, but many amalgamations have led to there being relatively few large organisations left.

Questions

1 In your opinion, which was the major step forward in economic growth in Britain's history, and why?
2 Discuss the main reasons for the appearance and disappearance of the gilds.
3 Was enclosure a good or bad thing for Britain?
4 Why did the agrarian revolution come about? Suggest the likely outcome for Britain, if it had happened 100 years later.

Chapter 5

Supply and demand analysis

Introduction

The first four chapters have tried to give a general impression of the subject matter of economics. In these earlier chapters certain facts have been assumed to be known in general knowledge. One such fact is basic supply and demand behaviour. Most people realise that if a shop suddenly reduces its prices, more goods will be sold. Conversely if the same shop doubles its original prices, it is likely to sell fewer goods under normal circumstances.

This chapter will delve more deeply into the workings of supply and demand analysis, and will show its uses in the economy of today.

Demand

Demand can be defined as the amount of a good or service that a person or society will buy at a particular price at a particular time.

A typical demand curve is shown in Fig. 5.1. When investigating demand curves, it is best if one can relate oneself to the consumer who may buy the goods. In Fig. 5.1 it can be seen that if the price was relatively high, at y_1, then demand would be relatively low, at x_1. If, on the other hand, the price

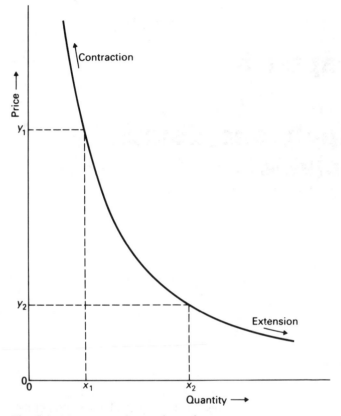

Fig. 5.1 Movements along a demand curve

Table 5.1 Washing machine sales

Unit price (£)	Number sold (1000s)
260	1.35
250	1.35
230	1.6
200	2.5
180	3.85
170	5.0
159	8.0

were to drop to y_2, then the quantity demanded would rise to x_2. This movement, which can occur along a single curve, is known as contraction or extension, as indicated on Fig. 5.1.

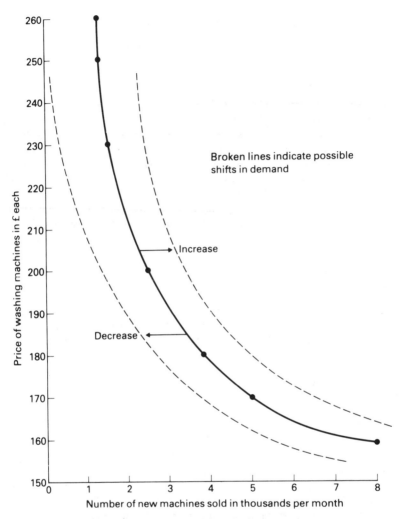

Fig. 5.2 The market demands for washing machines

The market demand for any good can be found by adding together the demand of all the separate consumers. For example, consider the number of people who would buy a new washing machine, if the prices of new machines were as shown in Table 5.1. These values are shown in graphical form in Fig. 5.2.

The workings of a single curve as in Fig. 5.1 assume that all external forces remain unchanged, and that only the price of the particular good in question changes. If certain outside influences are altered, then this could result in a 'shift' of the curve to the left or right of the original position, as in Fig. 5.2. This would indicate a decrease or increase in demand.

Explained below are several influences that could bring about these 'shifts'.

The price of other goods

Two types of relationships between goods exist, which can cause this movement. They are complementary goods, and competing or substitute goods. In the building industry, a good example of complements would be that of undercoat and gloss paint. Generally one is not bought or used without the other, and if for some reason the price of gloss paint suddenly doubled, people might not redecorate quite so often, hence the demand for undercoat would drop, although its price had not changed.

Wallpaper on the other hand could be classed as a substitute for emulsioned walls. If a revolutionary printing process suddenly halved existing wallpaper prices, then the demand for emulsion paint might drop, as more people would choose to wallpaper their rooms.

Change in a person's income

In general, an increase in a person's income leads to an increase in demand for many commodities that he now buys. Indeed, it may enable the consumer to buy goods he could not have afforded before. Certain goods, however, show a tendency for less to be bought when incomes rise; these are known as Giffen goods, and consist of inferior goods which would be replaced with more expensive goods.

Changes in tastes may cause very sudden changes in demand curves

This is particularly noticeable in the world of fashion. Taste is very often dictated by trendsetters, whether the area considered is clothes, car shapes, music, hairstyles, drinks or cigarettes. Whenever a new trend is set, by the appearance of a pop star or a member of the royal family in a certain mode of dress, then relevant demand curves may shift dramatically. Advertising, particularly on the television, can often persuade people to buy various goods and this again can affect the demand for the good being advertised, or its competitors.

New technologies

Very often, new discoveries make other traditional products obsolete, hence the demand for the old products almost disappears. An example of this would be the development of the electronic calculator. The calculator has almost completely replaced the slide rule, as it can perform many more functions much quicker than a slide rule. Although slide rules can still be bought, not many are sold, even though their cost is usually less than that of a calculator.

Population changes

Here there are two factors to consider. If total population increases, or decreases, then for the majority of goods, the demand will follow.

The other change likely to occur is a varying of the age structure of the population. This may for example vary over a period of years, from a mainly young to a mainly old population. Whilst this would not affect some goods, such as foods, it would affect demand for types of clothes and toys.

Taxation, and the distribution of income

Taxation, as will be discussed later, is imposed by government either to raise revenue, or to try and cut back demand. There may be times when it is thought to be in the nation's interest to reduce sales for example on imported goods.

Taxation can also be used to try to correct inequalities of income distribution. The object is to level out the incomes of the very rich, and very poor, by taxing the rich heavily, and giving subsidies to the lower-income groups. Consequently, the poor now have more money to spend, and so demand for the goods that they buy should increase.

Elasticity of demand

This is an indication of the responsiveness of demand to a change in price, and can be measured by:

$$\text{Elasticity of demand} = \frac{\% \text{ change in demand}}{\% \text{ change in price}}.$$

As the slope of the demand curve is negative, the result always comes out negative. So for convenience, the answer is always multiplied by -1.

A figure greater than 1 is said to be relatively elastic.
A figure of 1 is said to have unity elasticity.
A figure less than 1 is said to be relatively inelastic.

Consider the graphs of Fig. 5.3.

Figure 5.3(a) shows a situation where people continue to buy the same amount, whatever the price, hence demand does not alter, it is perfectly inelastic. Figure 5.3(e), on the other hand, shows a very improbable situation where the demand would alter infinitely, although there is no change in price. This shows perfect elasticity. Figures 5.3(b), (c) and (d), show intermediate stages of demand, the sort of demand more likely to be seen in practice.

Consider Fig. 5.4. Assume the price drops from £20 to £19, the elasticity is given by:

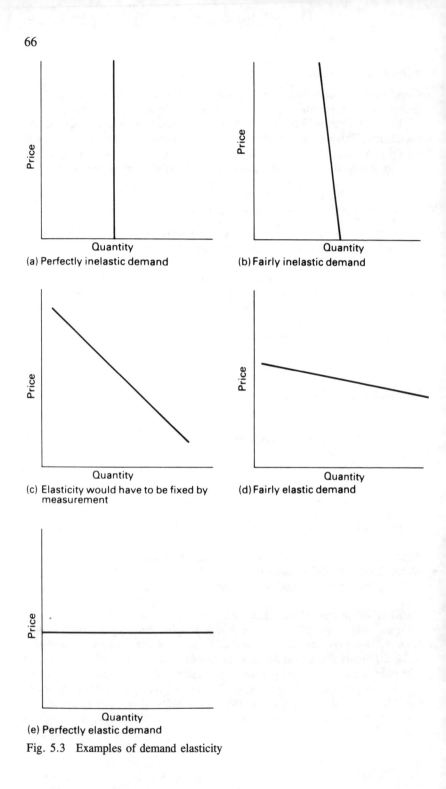

(a) Perfectly inelastic demand

(b) Fairly inelastic demand

(c) Elasticity would have to be fixed by measurement

(d) Fairly elastic demand

(e) Perfectly elastic demand

Fig. 5.3   Examples of demand elasticity

$$\frac{\%\ \text{change in demand}}{\%\ \text{change in price}}$$

$$\%\ \text{change in demand} = \frac{22.50 - 25}{22.50} \times 100 = -11\%$$

$$\%\ \text{change in price} = \frac{20 - 19}{20} \times 100 = 5\%$$

$$\text{elasticity} = \frac{-11}{5} \times -1 = 2.2$$

Elasticity can also be worked out on price increases. Assume the price rises from £19 to £20. Again the formula is used, being careful not to confuse the initial and final figures:

$$\%\ \text{change in demand} = \frac{25 - 22.50}{25} \times 100 = 10\%$$

$$\%\ \text{change in price} = \frac{19 - 20}{19} \times 100 = -5.26\%$$

$$\text{elasticity} = \frac{10}{-5.26} \times -1 = 1.9$$

Note, there is a difference between the two figures. If elasticity is calculated for a price drop from £5 to £4 the figure for elasticity is about 0.21.

From the wide variations of these figures it can be seen that to determine accurately the elasticity of demand of a good, the exact range over which we are interested must be specified together with the direction of movement. Most demand lines are curves, not straight lines, and a curve such as in Fig. 5.2 would tend to have a more constant elasticity than the straight line of Fig. 5.4. For the majority of situations, it is only necessary to know that a good is either relatively elastic, or relatively inelastic; precise figures are not needed.

It has been shown how elasticity can be calculated, but to what purpose can it be put?

(a) A producer can determine whether his total revenue is likely to increase, or decrease, following a change in price. Consider Fig. 5.4. A price drop from £20 to £19 would cause a revenue increase of £25, i.e. 19 × 25 = £475, against 20 × 22.50 = £450. A price drop from £5 to £4, however, would cause a revenue drop of £50, i.e. 4 × 62.50 = £250, against 5 × 60 = £300. It can be seen that a price drop when a good is relatively elastic causes an increase in revenue, whereas a price drop when the good is relatively inelastic causes a reduction in revenue, and vice versa.

(b) At budget time, the Chancellor of the Exchequer invariably bears in mind the elasticity of goods, when deciding whether or not to increase indirect taxes. The argument follows similar lines to that in (a) above. A tax increase means an increase in price, and on a relatively inelastic demand, this means an increase in revenue for the government.

68

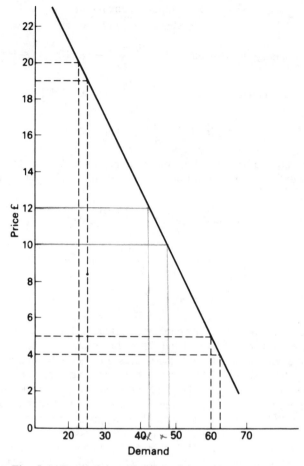

Fig. 5.4 Determining elasticity of demand

Factors affecting elasticity of demand

1. The proportion of income spent on a commodity. For example, in the average household, little would be spent on paper tissues, so if the price doubled, the effect on the family budget would be negligible. Consequently demand probably would not change. However, if the price of clothes suddenly doubled, then as a larger proportion of income is spent on these goods, demand would have to be cut back.

2. The level of consumers' income. A person who enjoys a large income is more likely to treat most of his purchases as inelastic, because he has plenty of money, and is able to easily afford them. A person on a lower income tends to treat the majority of his purchases as elastic. If he cannot afford them he obviously does not buy them.

3. Does the good have any substitutes? Goods which have no substitutes will tend to be inelastic in demand. An example of this is glass, which has no cheap substitute; people have to buy glass if they want windows in their buildings. Goods which have many substitutes however, tend to be elastic in demand, for if the price of this type of good increases, the consumers will buy a substitute.

4. Is the good a luxury or a necessity? In general, goods which are neccessities, such as food, have to be purchased, and so are inelastic. Luxury goods, such as caravans, boats, freezers etc. can be done without, so that if the funds are not available they will not be bought. Luxury goods then are elastic in demand.

5. Is the good a single use or durable use commodity? In other words, is the good used once only, like food, paint or fuel, or is it used many times like tools? When a single use good has been used, then it has to be replaced, its demand is inelastic. With durable use goods, because they can still be used even when well worn they can if necessary be replaced less often; this gives them an elastic demand.

6. Is the good linked with a trend or habit? Many young people feel compelled to buy certain clothes, because they are in fashion. Therefore, over a relatively short period of time, the demand for green wigs, should they be in fashion, would be inelastic.

Certain goods are linked with habits, particularly alcoholic drinks, and tobacco. If people find it difficult to give up smoking or drinking, then these goods will tend to be inelastic.

Income elasticity of demand

This can be defined as an indication of the responsiveness of demand for a particular change in income:

$$\text{Income elasticity of demand} = \frac{\%\ \text{change in demand}}{\%\ \text{change in income}}.$$

The demand for luxury goods, i.e. cars, boats, caravans etc., obviously rises with an increase in income. They tend to have an elastic income demand. Basic foods such as potatoes and bread are required whatever a person's income, so are relatively inelastic.

Cross elasticity of demand

This is often used by manufacturers, to determine how complementary or competitive two goods are:

$$\text{cross elasticity of demand} = \frac{\%\ \text{change in demand of commodity X}}{\%\ \text{change in price of commodity Y}}.$$

Consider the following examples.

Example 1:   There are two commodities, A and B. The price of A doubles, which results in demand for B being halved. Are the goods complements or substitutes?

$$\text{The cross elasticity of demand} = \frac{-50}{+100} = -0.5.$$

(Negative figures always indicate complements.)

Example 2:   The doubling of the price of commodity X causes a doubling in demand of commodity Y. Again, are the goods complements or substitutes?

$$\text{The cross elasticity of demand} = \frac{100}{100} = +1.$$

(Positive figures always indicate substitutes.)

Example 3:   The price of good M is doubled, this makes no difference to demand for commodity N. What is the relationship between the two goods?

$$\text{Cross elasticity of demand} = \frac{0}{100} = 0.$$

(Zero figure indicates that the goods are totally unrelated, as one would expect.)

Supply

This can be defined as the amount of a good, or service, that producers will put on to the market at any particular price.

When analysing supply curves, one must think in terms of the producer, whereas with demand curves, one has to think in terms of consumers. A typical supply curve is shown in Fig. 5.5. From this graph it can be seen that the higher the price, the more will be supplied. There are two explanations for this:

(a) If a higher price can be realised for a product, then more profit can be made, therefore manufacturers want to turn out more products.
(b) As the selling price of a good rises, more firms are now able to produce the goods at this higher figure, whereas at a lower price they could not compete and so would not produce the goods.

With supply curves, as with demand curves, they can extend or contract, or they can increase or decrease, as in Fig. 5.6. An extension or contraction would be determined by the price charged for a commodity, whereas a decrease or increase would be brought about by changes in the conditions of supply. These may be due to the following cause.

1. A change in the prices of factors of production.   An increase in the prices of materials or labour, means that less manufacturers would be able to supply the good, whilst maintaining prices. This would result in the supply line shifting to the left: A decrease in factor prices would cause a shift to the right.

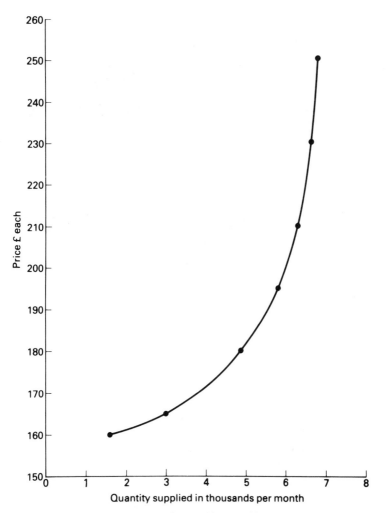

Fig. 5.5 Typical supply curve for washing machines

2. Farm products being affected by weather. Bad weather may result in farmers requiring greater prices per unit, to compensate for a smaller crop. In this instance, bad weather would result in a shift to the left. A good harvest, on the other hand, would result in a shift to the right as vast stocks of crops are sold off at low prices.

3. Advances in technology altering production methods. Very often, in industry, a new production process results in faster and cheaper production. This leads to an increase in supply, as goods can now be produced more cheaply than before, so that manufacturers make more profit than previously, at any particular price.

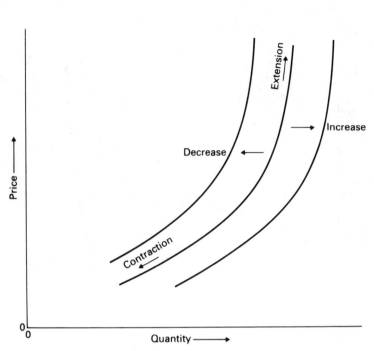

Fig. 5.6 Movement of supply curves

4. Taxes or subsidies. Should the government impose a tax on a product, the tax will often be paid initially by the producer, so that this in effect works the same as an increase in the factor costs, and results in a supply decrease.

A subsidy paid to the producer, however, results in a supply increase.

Elasticity of supply

This can be defined in a similar manner to demand elasticity. Elasticity of supply is an indication of the responsiveness of supply to a change in price, and can be written as:

$$\text{Elasticity of supply} = \frac{\%\ \text{change in supply}}{\%\ \text{change in price}}$$

As nearly all supply lines have positive slopes, the elasticity of most lines is positive, and again a figure greater than one would show a relatively elastic supply. A figure of one is unity elasticity, and a figure less than one denotes an inelastic supply. See Fig. 5.7.

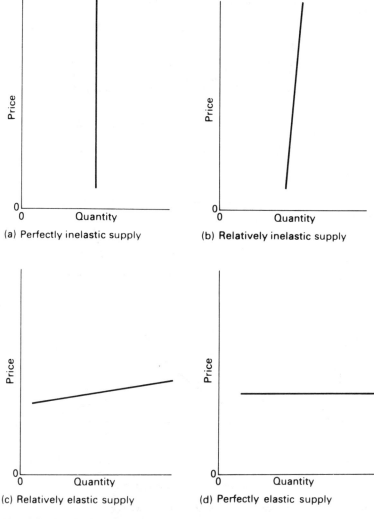

Fig. 5.7 Elasticities of supply

Elasticity of supply is determined largely by the ease with which producers can change their level of operations. Certain industries, for example the shipbuilding industry, require investment months, or even years ahead of actual production. Consequently it is very difficult to alter the level of production when goods take a long time to produce. Products with such long production periods have inelastic supplies, whereas when the production can be stopped or changed at short notice then the level of production can be altered to meet the prevailing circumstances quickly.

Fig. 5.8   Equilibrium price of washing machines

Equilibrium price

Equilibrium price comes about, as a result of the interaction of supply and demand. If Fig. 5.2, the demand curve for washing machines, and Fig. 5.5, the supply curve for washing machines, are combined, this gives Fig. 5.8. On this diagram, there is one point at which both sellers and buyers are satisfied. At the price of £175 the demand equals supply at 4400 machines per month. This point of intersection of the curves is known as the equilibrium point.

Over a period of time, the market situation adjusts automatically to an equilibrium price, given that certain conditions of perfect market competition exist. The idea of a perfect market assumes the following:

(a) The commodity produced is exactly the same as all other products of that type. Thus if a manufacturer produced kettles, then it is assumed that they are exactly the same as all other kettles produced. This cuts out any possibility of choice based on brand, colour or gimmicks.

(b) There is a large number of buyers and sellers: If this situation exists, then no one buyer or seller can influence the demand or supply of a particular product. If there were only one buyer, then he could dictate what price he would pay or how many he would buy. Similarly if there were only one supplier, then he could fix the amount of goods produced or the price at which he would sell.

(c) There is perfect market knowledge. By this is meant that all buyers and sellers have immediate knowledge of price movements, and supply movements. Thus, if, due to a surplus of stock, the price of a good were reduced, then the market as a whole is assumed to know this immediately, and there would be a sudden increase in sales.

(d) All commodities produced are perfectly mobile. This ensures that the previous assumption could be achieved, and that in a particular market only one price existed. In reality the majority of commodities are mobile. In the construction industry, however, it is just the opposite. At the present time in certain areas there is a shortage of dwellings, in other areas there is a glut. This is the main reason for the vastly different house prices in different parts of the country.

(e) Firms are free to enter or leave an industry. If a firm is making particularly good profits, then other firms will be attracted into the industry. If on the other hand a firm is making a loss, then it is free to cease operations in that industry, and seek a more profitable alternative.

(f) All factors of production are perfectly mobile.

Now that the assumed environment has been studied, it should be easier to understand the self-adjusting mechanism of the market. In Fig. 5.8, if it is assumed that the price of washing machines was fixed at £195 then the demand would be 2800 machines per month, but supply would be 5850 machines per month. Because there is an excess of the goods, the price would fall, there would be an extension in demand, and a contraction in supply, until the equilibrium point was reached. In practice, the speed with which the equilibrium point is reached is dictated mainly by assumption (c) above, the degree of perfection of market knowledge.

If it is now assumed that the price was initially set too low, say at £160, then the demand of 7650 machines would far exceed the supply of 1550. As demand was so much higher than supply, then the price would rise. As this happens, however, the demand will contract whilst the supply extends, until the equilibrium point is reached.

Fig. 5.9 The effect on price of a change in demand

The effect of changes in demand on the equilibrium point

In Fig. 5.9, there exists a steady market demand of 150 cast iron spiral staircases per month, at £500 each. As a result of a new television series in which such a staircase is often shown, a new trend has been set and demand has increased, and is now shown by demand line 2. As the same conditions of supply are still in existence, the supply line is unaltered. A new equilibrium point is eventually reached at a price of £700 for a quantity of 250 per month.

Conversely a decrease in demand might come about due to an amendment of the Building Regulations making such staircases illegal for new works, in certain situations. This demand drop is represented by demand line 3 on Fig. 5.9, and shows that with such a situation, there is a drop in price coupled with a drop in demand.

Fig. 5.10   The effect on price of a change in supply

The effect of changes in supply on the equilibrium point

In Fig. 5.10 the supply and demand situation for cast iron spiral staircases is again represented. Supply line 1 indicates the initial situation resulting in the sale of 150 staircases per month at £500 each.

Due to a technological breakthrough in the casting process, manufacturers are now able to supply more units at any particular price. This causes the supply to increase to supply line 2 resulting in more sales, but at a lower price. Note that demand conditions have not altered.

Alternatively, a decrease in supply could be brought about by a massive wage settlement of say 50 per cent being paid to the foundry workers. This results in less manufacturers being efficient enough to offer the units at a particular price. Supply line 3 demonstrates this, and shows that a drop in supply, coupled with an increase in price, would result.

Normal price and market price

The normal price is often termed the long-period equilibrium price, for it is that price at which demand will equal supply, in the long term.

Market price is the short-period equilibrium price and this price indicates short-term fluctuations in the market conditions. For example, there are occasionally scares that sugar will be in short supply. Imagine that as a result of political or climatic problems a possible shortage has been announced. The result may be panic buying, which in turn may result in a doubling of price. This high price would only be a short-term market price, for people would not, under normal circumstances, tolerate such a price.

Questions

1 Suggest two commodities that would fit approximately the demand curves for Figs. 5.3 (b), (c) and (d), and give reasons for your choice.
2 (a) From Fig. 5.4 determine the elasticity of demand for a price change from £12 down to £10.
  (b) At this point, is it elastic or inelastic?
3 (a) Determine graphically the equilibrium point from the figures given over the page.
  (b) A change in conditions causes a shift in demand which can be shown by including the following figures, on the graph.
    (i) Determine the new equilibrium point.
    (ii) Suggest reasons for the shift in demand.

Chapter 6

The use of supply and demand analysis

Introduction

Supply and demand analysis is useful, not only to producers or other parties engaged in trading, but also to government. By the adoption of various policies, government can help to guide:

(a) manufacturers in their choice of goods produced
(b) buyers in their choice of goods to consume
(c) importers and exporters in their choice of goods handled
(d) farmers and food producers in their choice of products grown

Fiscal control is the tool used to try to achieve these various policies, and this comprises the selective use of taxes and subsidies, in order to achieve certain objectives. All democratically elected governments, irrespective of which party is in power, have certain general or normative objectives, which are considered necessary in the present day, for the good of the nation and its population. These objectives cover the following areas, and some will be discussed in more depth in later chapters:

(a) improvement of living standards
(b) high level of employment
(c) ensuring a good balance of payments
(d) curbing of inflationary tendencies
(e) equalisation of the distribution of wealth

Supply and demand, and particularly elasticity analysis, can be used in many ways to help achieve the objectives above.

Consider the following examples.

The effect of taxation on commodities of different elasticities

Taxes on goods can be classified under two headings, *specific taxes*, which is where a fixed amount of tax is paid per unit, or *ad valorem* taxes, where a percentage of the price is added on as tax. A typical example of a *specific tax* is excise duty, which is payable on cigarettes, spirits and petrol. Value added tax on the other hand is a good example of *ad valorem* tax.

The effect of specific taxes

Consider the statistics in Table 6.1, which are put into graphical form in Fig. 6.1.

From the figures it could be deduced that a specific tax of £2 per item has been imposed, but the effect of the tax is not immediately evident. Figure 6.1, however, shows a very shallow demand curve, and if the elasticity is calculated between supply curves 1 and 2, that is from a price of £3.50 rising to £4.20, a figure of 1.60 is obtained, indicating an elastic demand around these prices.

The £2 tax on the selling price has in effect made fewer manufacturers able to supply goods at the existing price. Initially 7000 could be supplied at £3.50, but after tax only 3100 could have been supplied at £3.50. This meant that if 3100 were supplied, due to the shortage of supplies, prices would have risen to £4.90. This in turn would have encouraged more manufacturers to produce, which would cause prices to drop until a new equilibrium point E_2 was reached.

Table 6.1

Demand		Supply before tax		Supply after tax	
Price (£)	Quantity (1000s/wk)	Price (£)	Quantity (1000s/wk)	Price (£)	Quantity (1000s/wk)
6.00	1	0.4	1	2.4	1
4.50	4	2.5	5	4.5	5
3.50	7	4.0	8	6.0	8
3.00	9	6.1	12	8.1	12
2.50	12				

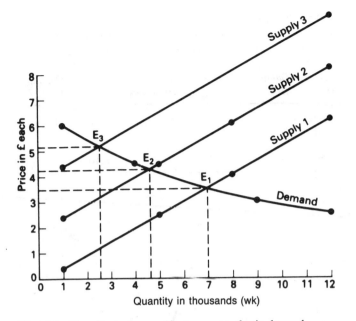

Fig. 6.1 The effect of a specific tax on an elastic demand

What is the effect as far as government revenue is concerned?

It would receive 4700 units at £2, which equals £9400/wk. If the government now anticipated adding a further £2 tax per unit, what would be its revenue then?

This would result in supply line 3, which would lead to E_3. The revenue would be 2600 units at £4 each which equals £10 400/wk.

Although the government tax revenue has increased, the much higher burden of tax is being borne by only about half the number of consumers that would have been involved had only £2 tax been imposed. Such a situation also poses other problems. If E_3 were the new equilibrium point, then only 2600 units would be needed, instead of the original 7000. This reduction can only normally come about by redundancies. Thus the action of adding £4 tax would go against one of the government's basic objectives, for it would reduce employment.

The difference between supply line 1 and 2 measured vertically is the £2 tax. The difference between E_1 and E_2 measured vertically is only £0.70. Although the government gets £2 tax per unit, only 0.70 comes from the consumer, the other £1.30 is added to the supplier's production costs. Producers then bear the burden of the majority of the tax. From the above it can be seen that there are several problems with imposing a specific tax on an elastic demand.

Consider now another set of statistics (Table 6.2) which again are reproduced in graphical form, this time as Fig. 6.2.

This product has the same supply lines as Fig. 6.1, it also has the same initial

82

Table 6.2

Demand		Supply before tax		Supply after tax	
Price (£)	Quantity (1000s/wk)	Price (£)	Quantity (1000s/wk)	Price (£)	Quantity (1000s/wk)
8.00	5	0.40	1	2.40	1
5.50	6	2.50	5	4.50	5
3.50	7	4.00	8	6.00	8
0.50	9	6.10	12	8.10	12

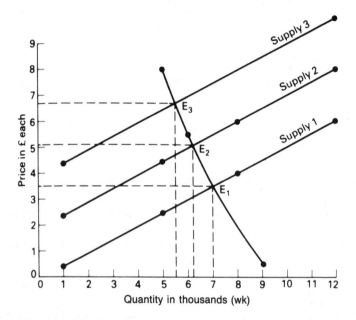

Fig. 6.2 The effect of a specific tax on an inelastic demand

equilibrium of 7000 units at £3.50. If the elasticity is worked out, however, between E_1 and E_2 it will be seen to be relatively inelastic.

What difference will this make to the arguments from the previous example?

From Fig. 6.2, it became evident that the imposition of the tax has resulted in only a slight reduction in demand, compared to Fig. 6.1, and much more of the £2 tax is now borne by the consumer, rather than the producer.

Government would raise revenue of 6200 at £2 which equals £12 400, which is considerably more than that raised in Fig. 6.1.

If the tax were raised to £4 per unit, the revenue would be 5500 at £4 which

Table 6.3 Summary of specific tax

On elastic demand commodities:	On inelastic demand commodities:
It causes a large contraction in demand.	It causes small contraction in demand.
Most of the tax is borne by suppliers.	Most of the tax is borne by consumers.
Tax is borne by relatively few people.	Tax revenue comes from many consumers.
Relatively small potential tax revenue.	Relatively large potential tax revenue.

equals £22 000. This massive revenue would result in only a relatively small drop in the quantity demanded and supplied, and so would not cause excessive redundancies.

Commodities with inelastic demands are much more likely to find themselves the targets of the Chancellor's budget policies than those with elastic demands, as the quantity demanded is less likely to change.

The effect of *ad valorem* tax

Figure 6.3 has the same demand line and initial supply line as Fig. 6.1. Instead of a specific tax of £2, however, the government has decided to operate a 50

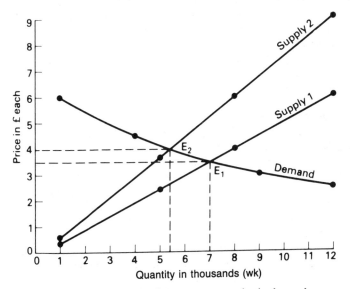

Fig. 6.3 The effect of *ad valorem* tax on an elastic demand

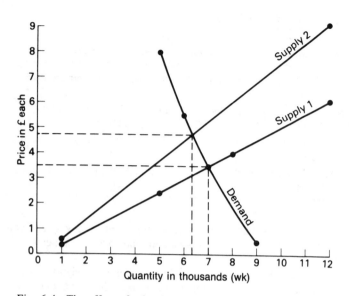

Fig. 6.4 The effect of *ad valorem* tax on an inelastic demand

per cent *ad valorem* tax. This results in supply line 2 of Fig. 6.3. This tax results in similar changes with respect to supply and demand to those of Fig. 6.1; there is, however, one major difference. With the specific tax, the same amount per unit was recovered as tax, irrespective of price. This resulted in the parallel supply lines of Fig. 6.1. With the *ad valorem* tax, whatever the price was originally, it is now 50 per cent greater. An advantage of the *ad valorem* tax for government is that, as the price rises, as it normally does over a period of time, so will the tax revenue. With the specific tax, however, there is no such automatic adjustment.

Figure 6.4 has an identical demand and initial supply line to those of Fig. 6.2, and again a 50 per cent *ad valorem* tax addition gives supply line 2. It will be observed that, added to the problems of tax on elastic goods discussed earlier, there is yet another disadvantage. With elastic demand commodities, there is a lower recovery of tax per unit than with inelastic demand commodities. In Fig. 6.3 tax per unit at E_2 is only £1.30, whereas in Fig. 6.4 the tax per unit is £1.60. It is essential that, when applying *ad valorem* tax to goods having elastic demand, a full study of the effects of the tax on price and demand should have been carried out. For example it might have been assumed that a commodity had a demand of Fig. 6.4, when in fact it more closely followed that of Fig. 6.3. Instead of the Chancellor realising a revenue of 6400 at £1.60 (£10 240), he would only have obtained 5400 at £1.30 (£7020), a considerable difference.

The effect of subsidies on supply and demand

A subsidy on a particular commodity has the effect of reducing the production costs. As stated previously this will result in a new supply line with a shift to the right.

Figures 6.5—6.8 show the results of a £2 subsidy per unit on various combinations of elastic and inelastic supplies and demands.

Figure 6.6 perhaps shows best the workings of a subsidy. Initially the equilibrium point is at E_1, but after being subsidised, the supply line drops £2 to supply line 2 which results in a new equilibrium point at E_2. It can be seen that the demand has increased from 5600 to 9700 per week and the total subsidy that the government will have to pay will be 9700 × £2 (£19 400). The consumers, however, do not pay £2 less, they do in fact pay only £1 less, the other £1 then must be kept by the producers. From studying Figs. 6.5—6.8 the following conclusions can be drawn.

(a) Figure 6.6, with elastic supply and demand, shows a fairly large drop in price, coupled with a large extension of demand. The more nearly perfect the elasticity of supply and demand is, the greater is the extension in demand.

(b) Figure 6.8, with elastic supply and inelastic demand, shows the greatest drop in price, coupled with a small extension of demand. To enable the full £2 subsidy to be passed on to the consumer, there would have to be perfectly inelastic demand and perfectly elastic supply.

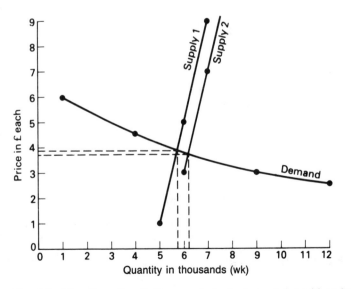

Fig. 6.5   The effect of a subsidy on an inelastic demand, but with an inelastic supply

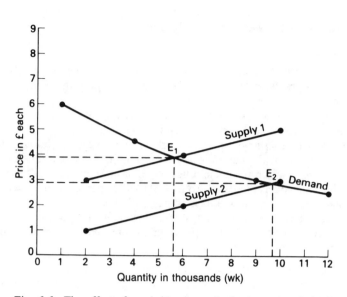

Fig. 6.6 The effect of a subsidy on an elastic demand and elastic supply

Fig. 6.7 The effect of a subsidy on an inelastic demand and inelastic supply

Uses of subsidies and taxes

Both taxes and subsidies can be used to help achieve the normative objectives stated earlier.

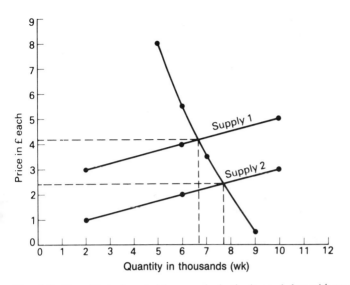

Fig. 6.8   The effect of a subsidy on an inelastic demand, but with an elastic supply

Subsidies can help curb certain economic problems; to help alleviate unemployment, demand could be stimulated, and conditions as in Fig. 6.6 would be sought to carry out the exercise effectively. In the past, subsidies have been introduced on agricultural products, in order to make Britain self-sufficient in times of war. See Chapter 16 for further details on current subsidies.

If subsidies were being used to reduce the cost of necessities and aid the poor, then situations like those depicted in Fig. 6.8 would be chosen.

In both the above cases, it will be seen that subsidies are of little benefit when used on inelastic supply curves.

Taxes are used by government for two main reasons:

(a) to raise revenue
(b) to cut back demand

Taxation is discussed more fully in Chapter 16, but the revenue raised by government is needed to pay for social services, health, defence etc. From time to time it becomes necessary for the government to increase its taxes. Ideally the government would look for situations resembling Fig. 6.2, where the demand is relatively inelastic. The more inelastic the demand, the greater will be the revenue obtained.

The taxing of luxury items tends to help redistribute wealth within the country. Rich people pay the tax, which means that the poorer sector of society needs to pay less tax. The problem here is that many luxury goods have very elastic demands, so that as more tax is imposed, demand rapidly falls.

Taxes may be imposed to cut back on demand for various reasons:

(a) To reduce home demand for a product, in the hope that the manufacturer will turn to exporting.

(b) To reduce consumption of socially undesirable goods, such as tobacco and alcoholic drinks. This group, however, tends to be very inelastic in demand, due to the habit-forming nature of the goods.

(c) To cut back on imported goods to help the country's balance of payments.

Questions

1 From the figures in Table 6.4, construct the supply and demand curves and find: (a) the total government revenue; (b) that total revenue borne by the consumer; (c) that total revenue borne by the supplier. A specific tax of £2 per item is added to the price of the good.

Table 6.4

Demand		Supply	
Price (£)	Quantity (1000s/wk)	Price (£)	Quantity (1000s/wk)
6	2	2	2
5	4	4	3
4	6	6	4

2 Construct the supply and demand curves from the figures in Table 6.5, and compare the results with those of Question 1.

Discuss the benefits or costs of the two situations with respect to (a) society in general; (b) government; (c) the suppliers. A specific tax of £2 per item is added to the price.

Table 6.5

Demand		Supply	
Price (£)	Quantity (1000s/wk)	Price (£)	Quantity (1000s/wk)
7.00	3.00	2.00	2.00
4.00	3.50	3.00	5.00
1.00	4.00	4.00	8.00

3   The government is trying to decide whether to subsidise the cost of all meat produced in the country. Discuss the possible outcome of such a policy with regard to (a) producers and consumers; (b) importers and exporters; (c) the society in general; (d) government.

Chapter 7

The clients and the different sectors of the construction industry in the UK

Introduction

The projects undertaken by the industry are very wide ranging, but can be classified by work type under two main headings:

(a) building
(b) civil engineering

The construction industry is perhaps one of the few industries that encompass such widely differing sizes of job, such as the replacing of a roof slate, to the building of a multi-storey office block or motorway. In size of firm, again there is a great variation between, at the one extreme, many sole traders who concentrate mainly on local maintenance work, to the other extreme of national organisations whose turnover is measured in millions of pounds.

There are many aspects of the industry that could be analysed, and in this chapter five will be looked at:

- the sectors of the industry as defined by type of work
- the size of firm

- the trade of firm
- the clients of the industry
- the gross domestic fixed capital formation

The classification of sectors

The construction industry can, as has already been stated, be split into building and civil engineering. It is necessary, however, to divide the industry down further in order to analyse more accurately current trends in construction activity.

One system of sector classification is that used by the Department of the Environment (DOE) in their quarterly publication *Housing and Construction Statistics*, which gives current output figures for the industry.

The headings are as follows:

1. New work:
   (a) public housing
   (b) private housing
   (c) other new work
      (i) industrial
      (ii) commercial
   (d) other new work − public
2. Repair and maintenance:
   (a) housing − public
   (b) housing − private
   (c) other work − public
   (d) other work − private

The *public sector* can be defined as any public authority, such as local authorities, nationalised industries, new town corporations etc.

The *private sector* is any private owner, developer or private organisation.

Industrial work would encompass such projects as factories, warehouses, chemical treatment plants etc.

Commercial work includes work carried out on shops, offices, farm buildings, dance halls etc.

Table 7.1 shows the output of the various sectors over the last eleven years, but with all work priced at 1985 prices. This allows comparison of the actual amount of work carried out.

If a particular year is analysed, say 1991, the various sectors can be compared by analysing their outputs.

Total construction output was approximately £31.88 billion, at 1985 prices (in this book 1 billion is taken as 10^9). Total new work was approximately £18.63 billion, with maintenance work at £13.25 billion.

Therefore new work represents:

Table 7.1 The value at output of the construction industry at 1985 prices £ million

| Year | New housing | | Other new work | | | All new work | Repair and maintenance | | | | All repair and maintenance | All work |
| | Public | Private | Public | Private | | | Housing | | Other work | | | |
				Industrial	Commercial		Public	Private	Public	Private		
1981	1366	3029	3706	2453	2724	13 278		5892	3913	2059	11 863	25 141
1982	1140	3482	3866	2202	3097	13 788		5858	3870	1955	11 683	25 470
1983	1210	4174	3943	1981	3169	14 478		6247	3947	1975	12 170	26 647
1984	1107	4036	4002	2443	3316	14 904	6577		3939	2118	12 633	27 536
1985	918	3848	3786	2848	3520	14 921	2993	3816	3800	2321	12 930	27 850
1986	815	4294	3802	2610	3984	15 505	3049	4064	3606	2533	13 252	28 757
1987	868	4771	3603	3021	4707	16 970	3149	4423	3660	2820	14 052	31 022
1988	789	5312	3639	3463	5395	18 599	3250	4740	3642	3038	14 670	33 269
1989	754	4319	3832	3828	6818	19 551	3299	4892	3722	3220	15 133	34 684
1990	703	3371	4252	4013	7590	19 928	3293	4741	3784	3270	15 088	35 016
1991	607	2784	4517	4331	6397	18 635	2793	4110	3393	2954	13 249	31 884

Source: Housing and Construction Statistics

$$\frac{18.63}{31.88} \times 100 = 58.5\%$$

with maintenance representing 41.5 per cent.

These figures surprise many people, as it is generally not realised that over one third of all money spent in the construction industry is on repairs.

The rest of the sectors can easily be calculated, and can best be shown on a pie chart as in Fig. 7.1.

From Fig. 7.1 it can be seen that the largest sector is new private commercial work. Repairs to housing in total however would be larger than this as all DIY is excluded from these figures. Housing repair represents an important source of work. The housing sector overall, that is repairs and new houses, represents 32 per cent of the industry workload.

The figures from Table 7.1 can be plotted on graphs (Figs. 7.2 to 7.4) which show up any trends in the sector outputs. It should be remembered, however, that such graphs are only a representation of historical figures, and are open to many interpretations.

The sectors described above are the ones most often used when the industry is discussed. There is nothing to stop further division by more detailed analysis

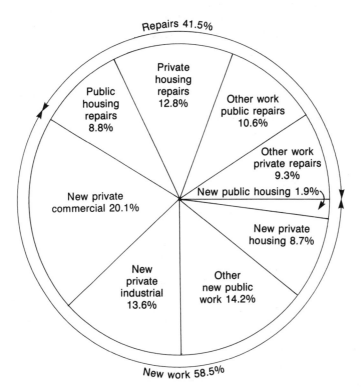

Fig. 7.1 Construction industry outputs by sector as a percentage of total work done in 1991

of the type of work. Indeed this is done in some DOE statistics tables, so that more detailed examination of both government and private expenditure can be undertaken.

The size of the firm

As the role of the industry is being portrayed, it is important to set the scene, by ensuring that the student has the basic information about the many building firms regarding their size and function.

Consider the figures in Table 7.2, which are taken from the housing and construction statistics.

(a) 96.6 per cent of construction firms employ less than 14 people. The number of firms employing over 13 men only constitutes 3.4 per cent of the total number of businesses.

(b) This 3.4 per cent of large businesses accounts for about 69 per cent of the industry's output, and about 56 per cent of the industry's workforce.

At this stage, students may be asking themselves 'Why are there so many small firms, and why so few large firms?' It is hoped that these questions will be answered when marketing and types of business organisations are dealt with later in the book.

Table 7.2 The size of construction firms and their outputs in the third quarter of 1991

Size of firm by number of operatives employed	Total employed thousands		Number of firms		Value of work done (£ million)	
1	94.5		103 169		809.3	
2–7	239.4	44%	92 116	96.6%	1648.0	31.3%
8–13	49.8		4 981		435.8	
14–24	61.0		3 429		615.8	
25–34	34.2		1 186		365.6	
35–59	49.0		1 100		556.2	
60–79	25.9		382		354.8	
80–114	35.4	56%	372	3.4%	472.3	68.7%
115–299	73.5		431		964.8	
300–599	57.0		137		835.6	
600–1199	46.0		58		810.8	
1200 and over	100.6		39		1369.2	
All firms	866.6		207 400		9237.6	

Source: Housing and Construction Statistics

Fig. 7.2 New housing and housing repair sectors

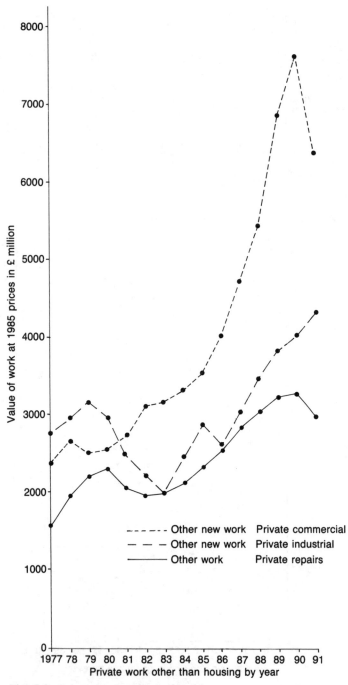

Fig. 7.3   Private work other than housing

Analysis by trade of firm

In the previous section, it was seen that in 1991 there were 207 400 firms in total. Table 7.3 gives a breakdown of this total by trade. This table at this stage may appear confusing, but the student should refer back to it during the reading of the rest of the text, where appropriate. The figures in Table 7.3 tend to show fairly well that the number of firms engaged in a particular trade is of course related to the demand for that type of work. Hence there will always be more general builders than floor and wall tilers, as people do not require the services of the latter very often.

Clients of the industry

Almost everyone in the country must at some time during their life be involved with the construction industry. It may be in the course of their work, or it may be in private life. The clients of the industry then are many and varied, and it again becomes necessary to categorise them. To a certain extent this has already been done in Table 7.1, where the two main client sectors are either public or private.

Much of the work for public bodies is subject to open or selective tendering, which tends to favour firms already specialising in the type of work under

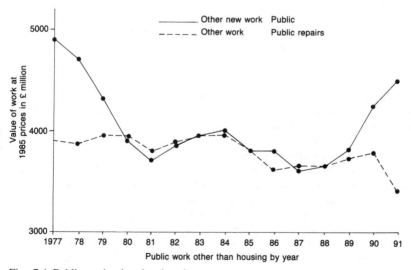

Fig. 7.4 Public work other than housing

Table 7.3   Analysis of construction firms by trade in third quarter 1991

By trade of firm	Number of firms	Work done (£ million)	Total employed (thousands)
General builders	76 991	2842.4	279.8
Building and civil engineering contractors	4 772	1789.0	116.7
Civil engineers	3 760	780.2	51.3
Plumbers	16 752	251.8	32.3
Carpenters and joiners	15 499	207.7	28.7
Painters	16 142	284.4	43.5
Roofers	7 722	251.6	25.1
Plasterers	4 761	80.2	11.4
Glaziers	6 435	238.6	24.8
Demolition contractors	635	27.4	3.2
Scaffolding specialists	1 597	126.4	16.2
Reinforced concrete specialists	999	51.6	5.2
Heating and ventilating engineers	9 375	566.6	50.3
Electrical contractors	21 020	800.0	86.2
Asphalt and tar sprayers	1 081	120.2	8.0
Plant hirers	4 579	181.3	20.3
Flooring contractors	2 033	70.8	6.7
Constructional engineers	2 640	188.7	16.7
Insulating specialists	1 281	79.7	10.0
Suspended ceiling specialists	1 659	53.8	4.6
Floor and wall tiling specialists	1 675	36.0	4.5
Miscellaneous	5 992	209 2	21.2
All trades	207 400	9237.6	866.6

Source: Housing and Construction Statistics

consideration. As much of this work is on a large scale, the firms doing public work tend to be of medium or large size.

In the private sector, the client may be a large national company, requiring a new factory or office block to be built, or it may be Mrs Jones from No. 37, wanting her front door eased. In this sector then, there is scope for all types and sizes of firms to operate.

In the civil engineering industry, however, perhaps 80—90 per cent of its work comes from the public sector, which can cause problems when the government cuts back on public expenditure.

Usually firms carry out work for many clients. There are of course exceptions to this, for instance: a civil engineering firm may specialise in carrying out roadworks for the Coal Board, or a small general builder may specialise in doing maintenance work at a large factory, where it was deemed uneconomical to have a direct maintenance labour force. The obvious problem of this dependence upon one client is summed up by the proverb, 'Never put all your eggs in one basket.'

The smaller building firms tend to carry out smaller works, and there are many reasons for this:

(a) Small firms have lower overhead costs, and so can do smaller jobs cheaper than the bigger firms, who have to carry higher overheads to cope with larger jobs.
(b) Small firms may lack the expertise or experience of carrying out the larger works.
(c) Finance is lacking for carrying out larger works.
(d) Personal attention by a small builder is appreciated by clients.

To sum up, in general terms: Small firms carry out small general works for private individuals and also highly specialised work such as glazing or air conditioning, for large public or private clients. At the other extreme, large firms tend to carry out work for large public and private clients.

The size and distribution of firms will be discussed further in Chapter 9.

Gross domestic fixed capital formation

Capital goods are those tending to have a durable nature. The formation of domestic fixed capital (DFC) can be said to be the amount of new factories, roads, plant, equipment and housing produced within the country.

From Table 13.2 of the Central Statistical Office *Blue Book* 1992 the following figures for Table 7.4 were extracted.

It can be seen from Table 7.4 and from Fig. 7.5, which is derived from it, that the construction industry plays a significant part in the formation of DFC.

Consider the year 1991.

The public sector incorporating all industries accounted for £12 761 million, the construction industry producing 81 per cent of this (£10 369 million).

The private sector had a total of £59 701 million of which the construction industry produced 41 per cent (£24 800).

Overall, however, the industry generally produces about 50 per cent of all gross domestic capital formation.

How important are these figures? It should be remembered that fixed capital formation represents an investment in the future of the economy of the country. This applies whether it is for the private sector in the form of houses or factories, or for the public sector in the form of new roads, town halls, schools etc.

It is hoped that all these projects will lead to greater output or greater efficiency within this country, and ultimately to a higher standard of living.

Future trends in gross domestic fixed capital formation

In the past, construction work for the government and other public bodies has

Table 7.4 Domestic fixed capital formation (£ million at 1985 prices)

	81	82	83	84	85	86	87	88	89	90	91
Private sector											
Dwellings	8 149	8 680	9 323	9 725	9 318	10 365	10 734	12 999	12 290	10 506	8 942
Other buildings	6 418	6 616	6 560	7 516	7 793	8 137	10 947	13 552	15 503	16 781	15 858
Tot. const. costs	14 567	15 296	15 883	17 241	17 111	18 492	21 671	26 541	27 793	27 287	24 800
Tot. cap. form. costs	35 762	38 556	38 724	43 419	47 550	48 937	55 807	66 361	70 046	66 647	59 701
Construction as % of tot. cap. formation costs	41	40	41	40	40	38	39	40	40	41	42
Public sector											
Dwellings	2 156	2 282	2 924	2 825	2 536	2 536	2 741	2 549	3 006	3 088	2 078
Other buildings	6 081	7 194	7 318	7 665	7 425	7 688	7 453	7 731	8 242	7 991	8 291
Tot. const. costs	8 237	9 476	10 242	10 490	10 061	10 224	10 194	10 280	11 248	11 079	10 369
Tot. cap. form. costs	12 671	12 555	14 752	14 615	12 803	12 876	11 946	11 034	12 951	13 817	12 761
Construction as % of tot. cap. formation costs	65	75	69	72	79	79	85	93	87	80	81
Overall for both sectors											
Construction as % of tot. cap. formation costs	47	48	49	48	45	46	47	48	48	48	49

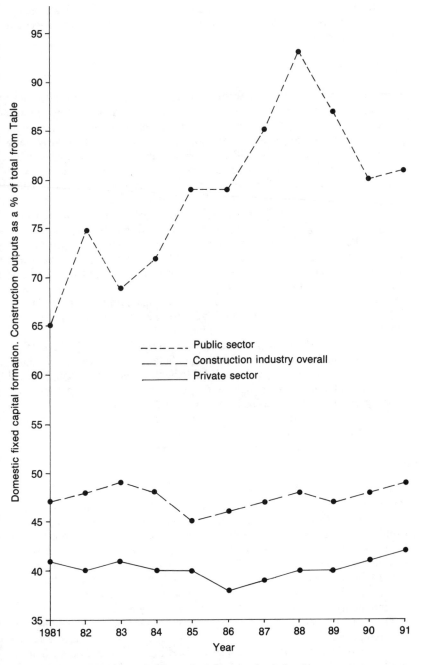

Fig. 7.5   Gross domestic capital formation. Construction industry sector as a percentage of total fixed capital formation

contributed a higher percentage to the DFC than work for the private sector. Will this continue to be the case? Several factors have to be taken into account when considering this.

Private housing

From the private housing viewpoint, in 1991 there are technically more dwellings in the country than households, so why do we need to build more houses? The answer may be that the houses might be the wrong size, or in the wrong location, to solve housing shortages. However, with a fairly static national population, the time will come within the next few years when there will possibly be a glut of houses. Some people would argue that that is what happened in the early 1990s. A proportion of the housing stock is badly neglected. This, together with increasing planning restrictions, has led to a growing interest in the refurbishment of older houses, to prevent the nation being left with a gigantic housing stock of dilapidated dwellings.

From the late 1960s the number of dwellings completed dropped until in the late 1980s completions were just over 200 000 units per year. Since then, with the recession in the United Kingdom, housing sales have dwindled. House prices in 1992 had dropped by approximately 20–25 per cent from the peak activity prices of 1988. The number of dwellings completed in 1980 was 235 530, in 1988 229 040 and in 1990 186 922. It is to be expected that numbers for 1991 and 1992 will continue to drop.

During the late 1980s people tended to increase their levels of debt on many commodities including housing. The period before the withdrawal of double interest tax relief on mortgages in 1988 (where an unmarried couple could both obtain tax relief on mortgage interest) caused a final burst of activity after which sales declined. Increasing unemployment during the early 1990s seemed to change society's attitude from one of spending to one of saving. It is hoped that the general reductions in interest rates in 1992 will encourage consumer spending in the economy, resulting in more demand for dwellings.

Public sector housing

Public sector housing is always a political hot potato, and is often impossible to discuss unless political policies are introduced. Broadly speaking, Conservative policy is to cut back on public housing, whilst Labour policy is just the opposite. If a 1–2 year delay is built into the system to allow for contract planning, or run-down time, the possible trends of the public housebuilding sector can be forecast reasonably accurately, depending upon which party is in power. Another political implication is that with both parties, housebuilding often increases slightly prior to a general election.

There are always likely to be low income or needy families seeking low-cost rented housing. The policy of the Conservative government is to reduce the ability of local authorities to construct dwellings, but to encourage housing development through housing associations. This is being encouraged by providing grants, from both central and local government, for registered housing associations. This is further discussed in Chapter 9.

Many local authorities are still paying the price for rash decisions made in the 1960s and 1970s concerning the erection of tower blocks. What with construction faults and social and vandal problems, many of the blocks are now having to be demolished only part way through their expected lifespan, to be replaced by low-rise housing.

Where old delapidated housing is being refurbished or replaced, much emphasis is now put on trying to maintain the existing environment and grouping of householders in order to reduce problems of upheaval.

Public sector other than housing

There is some uncertainty over this sector in the coming years. One would have expected that the tight rein on the purse strings of public spending would have reduced public expenditure, but from 1987 to 1991 it has increased each year. Should a Labour government return to power in the near future it is to be expected that there would be large injections of money into the economy via public construction work. Conservative policy, however, will tend to reduce public expenditure. Several major areas of work, particularly in the public utilities field such as electricity, water, gas and telephones now comes within the private sector.

Major expenditure areas still within the public domain such as education and health are unlikely to see large capital expenditure projects forthcoming. Transport projects should still continue at a reasonable level. There is much work to do on constructing and upgrading the road and rail infrastructure to link with the Channel Tunnel.

Large-scale works such as reservoirs, airports and motorway routes are becoming increasingly difficult to get approved by planning authorities due to the increasing power of the environmentalist lobby.

Private industrial and commercial sector

Many of Britain's traditionally strong industries such as shipbuilding, steelmaking and general engineering are tending to diminish under the competition from developing countries with lower labour costs. The outcome of this is that industry tends to have many smaller businesses of various types in a particular area, rather than one major employer.

This changing of emphasis has meant that work has been created by transforming large outdated factory complexes into estates of smaller landscaped industrial or business units. There are still large industrial employers blossoming who will need new premises. The decisions associated with when, where or if to build are more likely to be based on the size of European or central government grants available than on the more traditional reasons for location as discussed in Chapter 12. Perhaps with the coming of the Single European Market industries with good export potential will expand.

Two factors in particular are considered by industrialists, when contemplating expansion.

(a) A business investing in a new factory must have reasonable faith in the sales of its products. This is most likely to happen in a boom period rather than a recession.

(b) The new factory must be financially viable. High interest rates often cause the shelving of many new industrial projects, as they would not be profitable after paying high interest charges.

The accelerator principle

This is based upon the idea that a change in demand for durable capital goods leads to a greater change in activity in the industry supplying them.

For example a petrol distribution company has 500 petrol stations in the South of England division. These petrol stations are rebuilt or upgraded every five years by the construction industry. In order to assure a steady workload for the industry in this example, if 100 are rebuilt each year then after five years all 500 will have been rebuilt and we can start rebuilding again.

From Table 7.5 it can be seen that the demand for petrol stations is stable during the first two years so that the only work for the construction industry is the replacement of those due for rebuilding. However, in year 3 there is a demand for 10 extra stations or an extra demand of 2 per cent. This results in 110 stations being constructed − 100 rebuilt ones plus 10 new ones; this, however, represents an increase in construction activity of 10 per cent on the previous year. In year 4, although there is an extra demand for 10 more stations, or a change in demand on the previous year of 1.9 per cent, this does not lead to any extra activity in the construction industry. In year 5, however, there is an increase in demand of 9.6 per cent, which results in an increase of 36 per cent in construction activity based on last year's figures. Year 6 sees a drop of 7 per cent in demand leading to a reduction of construction activity of 60 per cent. In year 7 an extra demand of 7.5 per cent leads to extra construction work of 133 per cent.

If instead of rebuilding every five years the rebuilding was carried out every ten, then this would result in Table 7.6, where only 50 replacements would be carried out each year.

Table 7.5 Petrol stations required and level of activity of the supplying industry based on a ten-year lifespan

Year	Demand for petrol stations		Construction of petrol stations			
	Total required	% change on previous year	Replacements	Extra required	Total required	% change on previous year
1	500	—	100	—	100	0
2	500	—	100	—	100	0
3	510	2.0	100	10	110	10
4	520	1.9	100	10	110	0
5	570	9.6	100	50	150	36
6	530	−7.0	100	−40	60	−60
7	570	7.5	100	40	140	133

Table 7.6 Petrol stations required and level of activity of the supplying industry based on a five-year lifespan

Year	Demand for petrol stations		Construction of petrol stations			
	Total required	% change on previous year	Replacements	Extra required	Total required	% change on previous year
1	500	—	50	—	50	0
2	500	—	50	—	50	0
3	510	2.0	50	10	60	20
4	520	1.9	50	10	60	0
5	570	9.6	50	50	100	67
6	530	−7.0	50	−40	10	−90
7	570	7.5	50	40	90	800

It can be seen from these figures that if the stations last twice as long before needing rebuilding, the steady replacement workload is at a much lower level. If any slight changes in demand are superimposed on this lower level of activity it leads to much greater fluctuations in construction. It can be seen that the longer goods last, the greater the fluctuation is likely to be in the industry supplying them.

This particular phenomenon is important to the construction industry, because the products of the industry do last a long time, typically 50−70 years for many buildings, which is much longer than the examples shown here. Slight changes in demand caused by economic triggers − for example interest rate changes or recession − can lead to wildly fluctuating output levels within the industry. The accelerator is one of the major reasons for the stop − go problem in the construction industry.

Direct labour organisations

Until the 1980s most local authorities ran direct labour non-profit-making departments to carry out maintenance on local authority properties. With the increasing push of privatisation by the Conservative government most maintenance contracts are now put out to tender. This means that local authorities who have retained direct labour organisations may still obtain the work, but only if their prices are competitive with private industry. The tendering system removes two problems inherent in the old system. Without tendering many LADLOs were inefficient and poorly managed, leading to extra costs for the taxpayers. The old system was also criticised by the construction industry as it took much work away from businesses which could have carried out the work quicker and more cheaply. In some authorities DLOs still exist and flourish, but as can be seen from Tables 7.7 and 7.8 the proportion of work carried out by them has reduced considerably.

There are certain general advantages and disadvantages of DLOs as follows:

Table 7.7 The value and proportion of work undertaken by LADLOs in 1985 at 1980 prices (£ million)

	Public new work			Public repairs			Total
	Housing	Non-housing	All work	Housing	Non-housing	All work	
Undertaken by LADLOs	24	179	203	717	1153	1870	1356
Total work done by construction industry	750	3407	4157	1610*	2597	4207	8367
% of total work load carried out by DLOs	3.2	5.2	4.9	44.5	44.4	44.4	16.2

Source: Housing and Construction Statistics
* Estimated

Table 7.8 The value and proportion of work undertaken by LADLOs in 1991 at current prices (£ million)

	Public new work			Public repairs			Total
	Housing	Non-housing	All work	Housing	Non-housing	All work	
Undertaken by DLOs	4.1	38.6	42.7	349.1	306.7	655.8	698.5
Total work done by construction industry	810	5772	6582	3964	4807	8771	15353
% of total work load carried out by DLOs	0.5	0.7	0.6	8.8	6.4	7.5	4.5

Source: Housing and Construction Statistics

Advantages of DLOs

(a) Direct labour should in theory be more economical, by at least the amount of the profit margin, as their prime aim is to provide a service, not to make a profit. Profit is therefore not included in their costings.

(b) With a workforce totally under one's control, greater flexibility is possible, plus faster reaction to emergency work.

(c) Operatives ultimately acquire an intimate knowledge of the buildings upon which they work.

(d) The management is more able to ensure that operatives carrying out the work have been properly trained up to a certain standard.

(e) There is no delay whilst contracts and/or specifications have to be produced to enable private contractors to tender.

Disadvantages of DLOs

(a) There is no profit motive, therefore in many organisations there is little incentive to maximise efficiency.

(b) There may be periods when there is little work for the operatives to do.

(c) It often works out dearer than if a private contractor is employed, due to inefficiencies.

(d) A direct labour force requires the provision of back-up facilities of stores, workshops, vehicles, plant etc. plus administrative staff.

Generally DLOs are used for general non-specialised work, where a fairly even flow can be arranged, within a reasonably small geographical area.

Trade cycles

In all economies, there tend to exist trade cycles. In the past, many statistics have been studied, and figures produced, to try to validate the existence of a regular trade cycle, with a period of from 7 to 11 years.

It is important to realise at the outset that there is no such thing as a regular trade cycle which will repeat itself with unfailing accuracy every few years. Nearly all fluctuations leading to the occurrence of trade cycles have been caused by numerous different external factors outside the control of industry generally.

Consider the following, which are some of the factors likely to lead to fluctuations.

Government action

This may affect the construction industry either directly or indirectly, as follows.

Direct effects on the construction industry

From Fig. 7.1, public work accounted for 35.5 per cent of all work carried out by the industry in 1991. The government therefore has a large say in how much work the industry will be allocated, and it could reduce considerably the output of the industry if no new government or LA contracts were issued. This, however, is very unlikely to happen, as the government is frequently reminded by employers' associations of the problems caused by government stop—go policy.

The construction industry is therefore one of the first to suffer during times of recession. There are, however, problems for government with the operation of a stop—go policy. Governments are unlikely to stop work on projects already under construction, and as most public works tend to be large-scale, long-duration projects, little effect will be felt for possibly 12—18 months, until the contracts have been completed. A longer time lag may be experienced when the government wishes construction activity to increase. The design functions will become overloaded with work and thus the design and planning stages would not be able to cope. Added to this is the problem of planning permission delays and the actual tendering procedure. This could again lead to a 12—18 month period from the initial authority to proceed, to the placing of the contract. Here another point should be considered. The turnover of work is very slow during the early stages of a contract, and so a marked upturn in construction activity may not become apparent until 12 months after a job has started. This means two years after the government has taken off 'the brake'.

Indirect effects on the construction industry

Government can affect private construction development indirectly by the application of fiscal and monetary policies. These are considered fully in Chapter 15 and 16, after the workings of such policies have been studied.

Reasons for government action

There are infinitely many possible reasons for government implementing policies likely to affect the industry, but a few examples are:

(a) The country may be involved directly or indirectly in a war which would affect trade.
(b) Economic policies of other governments might affect the level of imports to, or exports from, this country.
(c) Energy factors, either the discovery of new reserves within the country, or the cutting off of supplies by other governments, often results in changes of policies.
(d) Effects of inflation.

Demands on industries, leading to the application of the accelerator

It was seen earlier in the chapter how a change in demand for petrol stations can lead to a greater change in the output of the construction industry which supplies them. It can be seen that if this were extended over many industries whose boom periods coincided, the construction industry might be considerably overworked at these times. Conversely, a small change in demand downwards in the industries concerned would lead to a considerable recession in the construction industry.

Increasing propensity to save

During a recession, people tend to save money rather than spend it. This tends to exacerbate the trough of a depression, and so increases the period of the depression. See later chapters on Keynesian policies, and the multiplier.

Questions

1 Why, when old houses can be modernised or refurbished, do we tend to pull down and replace old factories and warehouses, rather than adapt them?
2 If the country ever reaches the situation where very few new houses are required, will the value of property still tend to increase annually, or will it tend to depreciate, as a new car does now?
3 In which country would you think the accelerator principle is most likely to operate, and why:
   (a) a country with a very stable economy, good standards of living, and a slowly increasing relatively high national income?
   (b) a country with a fairly volatile economy, fluctuating standards of living and widely varying national income?
4 From Table 7.3, building and civil engineering contractors comprise 2.3 per cent of the firms in the construction industry, and yet they carried out 19 per cent of the total value of work. Painters comprise 7.8 per cent of the firms in the industry and yet they carried out only 3.1 per cent of the total value of work.
   Discuss these statements.

Chapter 8

The European construction industry

Introduction

The new Single European Market has brought a new challenge to the construction industry not only of the UK but to many of the other European countries as well. Many large national firms will now be seeking markets further afield in order to improve their turnover and hopefully their profit.

Some countries, notably Britain and France, already have many large companies that seek work across the world.

The rate and system of development of the European construction industry depends upon several factors. Companies wishing to gain work in other countries must know clearly:

(a) the tendering, contractual and legal system of these other countries
(b) the different methods of becoming involved in overseas markets
(c) the competition expected from other countries and the potential market within each market

Factors (a) and (b) are considered below; factor (c) can be seen within the brief notes concerning each country which follow.

Operating systems within the different countries

The construction industry within the European Community can be split into four groups.

1. *The UK and Ireland.* These two countries have similar procedures within the industry and legislature. There is great emphasis on legally watertight contracts for work carried out. The traditional contracting system involves an independent professional paid for by the client; either an engineer for civil engineering work, or an architect for building. In the UK quality often takes second place to price, when choosing between contractors.

2. *Germany, Denmark and the Netherlands.* The procedures which have to be followed within these countries are much more formal and are stricter than those in the UK. Much more emphasis is placed on quality. There is less legal wrangling over contracts as work is carried out more on a personal basis. Working conditions and wages are more strictly laid down than in the UK. In order to perform well in these countries good personal contacts are essential.

3. *France, Belgium and Luxembourg.* Like the previous model, the industry within these countries has very formal procedures which to the outsider can seem extremely bureaucratic and political, leading to much frustration at times.

   There tends to be less emphasis on consistant high quality, but this is still looked for, depending upon the type of contract used. In many areas ten-year building insurance against faults is compulsory and this could present difficulties for contractors wishing to work in France as they need to get qualification for this insurance.

4. *Spain, Italy, Greece and Portugal.* Tendering and planning procedures are highly regulated, involved and confusing and outsiders may find them difficult to contend with.

   Government procedures are very bureaucratic and can operate extremely slowly. In some areas there is much less emphasis on quality of the product.

The development of overseas business

There are four ways in which a company can be involved in business activities in overseas countries.

1. *Joint ventures with foreign companies.* This usually involves collaboration between two or more companies where each business has a particular expertise in certain fields and where by combining forces they can take on wider forms of construction activity.

2. *The takeover of foreign businesses.* It is often difficult to simply set up

a new contracting division in another country. As can be seen from the previous sections there are many differences between the operating procedures within the different countries. One solution to this is for the UK company to take over or become part owner of the other European company. This can be achieved by taking over the company completely or by becoming a significantly large shareholder in the other company.

3. *Specialist activities.* Joint ventures as described above occur where two or more companies take on a more or less equal responsibility for a contract. There are many contracts, however, where sub-contract specialists are required, either on a consultancy basis or where actual physical construction has to be carried out. It is perhaps in this area that the largest amount of international activity between companies in the construction industry exists. It enables markets for work to be expanded to other countries, while the difficulties of contract procurement and dealing with local bureaucracy is left in the hands of the main contractor, who is used to dealing with these problems.

4. *Competing with Continental European contractors.* The final method is by competing directly with Continental European contractors on their home ground. In order to do this it is essential to have a full working knowledge of the operation of the industry within the new market. It is usually necessary to have experienced employees who can direct the operations and negotiate with local officialdom to smooth the road to success. Even so there may be some countries where it is very difficult to obtain work by this method due to the 'old boy network' being particularly strong.

The various countries of the European community

Spain

Population 40 million people
The construction industry consists of very few large companies and many small companies.

Spain has possibly the greatest potential of all the EC countries in terms of construction growth. It is by no means the largest market, but it has shown the greatest growth record in recent years as its economy develops. Civil engineering is seen as the fastest developing sector.

United Kingdom

Population 57 million people
There tends to be a large proportion of small companies with relatively few large ones. Generally construction tends to be more profitable in the UK than elsewhere in the EC.

The UK construction industry's output is much more volatile than the other members of the EC and the down turn during 1990–93 has caused many liquidations in small and medium companies and a reduction or even abolition of profit margins.

Traditionally, although many of the biggest construction companies are based in the UK, there has been a general reluctance to seek work overseas. There has, however, been little reluctance on the part of overseas competitors seeking work in the UK. There has been a gradual reduction over the years in investment in training, which has led to a shortage of skilled workers in many areas.

The Netherlands

Population 14.7 million people
The Netherlands has a fairly low population total but has the highest population density in the EC.

The construction business is made up of very few large companies, the majority being small.

The industry is stagnant in most sectors but growth is expected in the area of environmental engineering and infrastructure upgrading.

Belgium

Population 10 million people
The vast majority (over 99 per cent) of construction businesses employ fewer than 20 people. There are very few large companies.

There is little public sector housing in Belgium and little being constructed at the present time. There is a considerable increase in private sector housing.

Due to Belgium having a central geographical position within the EC, industrial and commercial interests are continuing to develop, thus creating much construction work. Environment issues are starting to come to the fore, indicating the potential for more construction activity.

There are likely to be difficulties for outside companies trying to enter the Belgian market for the following reasons:

(a) Profit margins are generally low.
(b) Heavy government debt means that there are few public sector contracts.
(c) Confusion exists over different legislation in different areas.

Denmark

Population 5.1 million people, 30 per cent of whom live in Copenhagen
There are few relatively large companies with many smaller local based companies. At present there is an excess of skilled labour due to the decrease in output of the industry. There seems little scope for increasing output in the building sector in the short term, but investment is expected to grow in the civil engineering field.

Portugal

Population 10.3 million people
Portugal is one of the most underdeveloped countries within the EC. As such there is much scope for construction work in all sectors. In particular there are detailed plans for improving infrastructure and also to develop the tourist industry.

The construction businesses tend to be small, dealing on a local basis. Hence they are not big enough to move into other EC countries.

Greece

Population 10 million people, 38 per cent of whom live in Athens
Portugal and Greece are the two poorest countries in the EC in terms of Gross Domestic Product (GDP) per capita.

Greece at present has an extremely small construction market at 0.5 per cent of all EC construction.

Because of the economic problems in Greece there is unlikely to be much increase in public sector or other construction projects.

Ireland

Population 3.5 million people, 1 million of whom live in Dublin
The general economy is still very dependant upon agriculture, with the majority of large manufacturing concerns being owned by overseas companies. Construction activity had been declining up to 1988, but is expected to increase, particularly in the non-residential and civil engineering field.

Luxembourg

Population 400 000 people
It is the smallest country within the EC with most contracts being carried out by foreign contractors and consulting firms. There is unlikely to be much increase in demand for construction work.

France

Population of 56 million people
The industry has a few large internationally based contractors with the majority of the remainder being medium-sized regionally based companies.

Since 1988 much investment has been put into improving training to provide a more highly skilled labour force.

Like Belgium the central geographical position should give France a strong position within the EC.

Italy

Population 57 million people
There are two apparent regions within Italy. The industrialised wealthy north with a population of 38 million and the less developed south with a population of 19 million.

The vast majority of construction businesses are small locally based family owned concerns with very few large organisations. This predominance of family owned businesses, together with high levels of bureaucracy which exist in places, makes it difficult for outside companies either to buy into Italian companies or to obtain work by tendering.

Germany

Population 79 million people
The German economy is going through a phase of considerable upheaval at the present time due to the reunification of the East and West sectors. Considerable problems exist in bringing together a large, wealthy, technically developed country with a heavily polluted, economically inefficient one.

Some of the problems tending to deter new development are:

(a) There are land ownership disputes, where people are filing ownership claims on parcels of land.
(b) Commercial operation between East and West is proving difficult to standardise.
(c) Large areas of polluted land now have to be decontaminated.
(d) Lack of infrastructure in the East causes transport delays.
(e) There is a severe lack of skilled labour, and investment needs to be put into education and training to make it competitive.

Despite these many problems, reunification is leading to much work for the construction industry. Output in the residential sector has increased latterly and should continue to increase due to a serious shortage of housing. On the civil engineering side there continues to be expansion in infrastructure and environmental technology.

Questions

1 Carry out your own research to find out which countries have shown a marked increase in construction work over the last few years. Discuss reasons why you think these increased outputs in the industry have occured.

116

Fig. 8.1 Value of EC construction output in 1990 (bn ECU)
(*Source*: Europe in Figures)

Figure 8.1 could be used as a basis for comparison.
2 Discuss what activities your own company, or a large national company, has in overseas markets.

Chapter 9

Markets and Marketing

Markets

What is marketing: indeed, what is meant by a market?

A market is said to exist where buyers and sellers are brought together, so that goods can be exchanged for money. In the construction industry, the market has to be defined with care. One may talk of the market for the services of the construction industry, in which case the products dealt with are all those produced by the different sectors of the industry. This includes housing — both private and public — schools, hospitals, industrial work, roads, etc.

Alternatively, one may talk of the markets for purpose-made joinery, or housing, or for road building.

Besides defining the market by product, it can also be classified by the type of client. This in its broadest sense could mean the different sectors as discussed in Chapter 7.

Yet another method of defining market is by location. For instance, a market could be:

(a) local
(b) regional
(c) national
(d) overseas

It can be seen then that there are three ways of defining market:

(a) by product

(b) by client
(c) by location

On studying the construction industry in depth, it is found that certain products tend to be purchased by certain clients, and that certain products fit into specific location definitions, as far as a single company is concerned.

From Fig. 9.1, it can be seen that builders specialising in maintenance work generally deal with individual householders, and because profit margins are fairly tight, and competition fierce, it is not worth their while venturing far afield for work. Their market, as far as location is concerned, is local.

At the other extreme, large civil engineering contractors who are looking for projects valued in £ millions are prepared to work anywhere in the country, or even abroad, provided it is profitable. These companies will be dealing with clients at the other end of the scale, i.e. domestic and overseas governments. Their location market will be national or international.

In between the extremes of the two examples given, there exist many medium-sized operations, but generally they all fit within the broad band as shown in Fig. 9.1.

Why should the pattern of Fig. 9.1 exist? The question of company size and location will be dealt with more fully in Chapters 12 and 13, but a brief discussion on the company's relationship with the market would help at this stage. Consider the two examples given earlier.

1. Maintenance work. It has often been said that a man can go into a local ironmongers, buy a few tools and set up in business as a builder doing

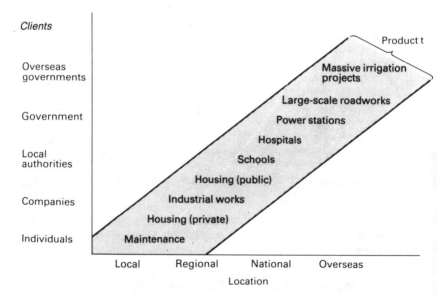

Fig. 9.1 The inter-relationship between the product market, the client market and the market defined by location

maintenance work. Without doubt, this still happens today, and such people often have little or no knowledge of the pricing of work, and often put in low prices in order just to obtain work. There are always such people in the small works area of building. Another group of people operating consists of moonlighters, who carry out work often without the taxman knowing, and so are able to charge less. In every locality there are many such people keeping down prices, and for this reason it would not be worth a bone fide builder travelling any great distance to obtain work, because his costs would be higher than those in the locality in which the potential work exists. With small jobs, a builder does not have expensive plant to keep working, indeed it is usual to hire much of the expensive equipment needed. He therefore has no worries about keeping plant working in order to get the maximum value from his investment.

From Chapter 7, it was seen that 95 per cent of the number of building firms in the country employ less than 14 operatives. The reason why there are so many small firms is linked to the type and amount of work undertaken by these firms. The smaller firms concentrate mainly on small works. As there is a large total value of this type of work, and as each small firm works strictly in a local market (often only in a radius of a few miles), then many firms exist.

2. Civil engineering. With the large civil engineering concern, the details are often in complete contrast to the previous type of business. National civil engineering companies employ many workers, and would normally come within the last category of Table 7.2, i.e. those employing over 1200 operatives. Only 39 such firms exist. Why are there so few? One of the main reasons again is the type and quantity of work. The type of work undertaken involves the use of very expensive plant, which, to be cost effective, has to be utilised to its utmost. Also, there is a large value of this type of work, but spread over very few contracts. There are therefore not the number of contracts to justify too many competitors, and because there are so few companies, their market location is national, i.e. they will consider work in any part of the country.

As these companies are so large, and because so much capital is tied up in them, the shareholders will ensure that they are efficiently run by competent managers. In normal times, there is little chance of a newcomer entering the market, undercutting prices drastically just to obtain work, for civil engineering is a field in which experience and contacts are a necessary prerequisite. The profit margins therefore tend to be fairly good. By the very nature of the work, there would be little difference in the costs of carrying out a contract in, say, South Wales, or in Edinburgh, as these sites often have all the specialist functions on site. Distance from head office tends to be immaterial.

Many national companies do, however, have regional depots, which may split up the country into four or five regions, but basically they are still national companies.

To define a company's market, it is necessary to bear in mind the following:

(a) the competition expected
(b) the degree of capital tied up in plant etc

120

(c) the management of the company, including expertise in particular fields
(d) the type of work
(e) the economic climate

Marketing

Marketing can be considered as the management function responsible for the determining, promoting and satisfying of the client's needs whilst meeting organisational objectives.

Business management can be led either by customers or profit. Profit orientation is indicated in Fig. 9.2.

When a business follows profit orientation, the profit for the organisation comes from increasing its sales.

Customer orientation involves extra stages to Fig. 9.2. In reality it is essential that marketing permeates all stages and areas of the business operation in order to gain optimum consumer satisfaction.

When a business follows customer orientation, the profit for the organisation comes from a customer-based method of operation. It is centred around putting the needs of the consumer before all decision-making processes. Within a customer- or market-orientated organisation all the activities are coordinated to ensure that the customers' needs are considered about what to produce, where it is sold and what means are used for production. There should also be a commitment by the organisation to meet the customers' needs more effectively than competitors.

Every business irrespective of size has a business plan. This may range from an unwritten set of ideas in the mind of the owner of a small business, to a formally presented document so essential for the larger company. Whether a marketing policy is included will depend upon whether the organisation is customer-orientated or profit-orientated.

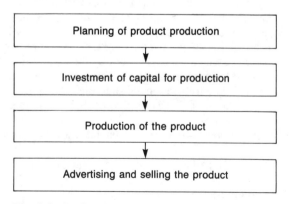

Fig. 9.2 Profit orientation within an organisation

Fig. 9.3 Customer orientation within an organisation

Why is a marketing policy necessary, and what should be included in it?

Many people consider marketing as a practice carried out with the sole intention of benefiting only the company itself. This is not so, for marketing can be said to benefit society in many ways, as follows:

(a) By providing products or services at the most economical prices, by the optimum allocation of the company's production factors.
(b) Greater company efficiency leads to greater profits, which flow back into society.
(c) Reducing business risk, thereby helping to ensure continuing employment.

A marketing policy which is formulated after a properly conducted investigation should help to guide the company into the most profitable markets.

Before a marketing policy is formulated, four areas, as indicated later on Fig. 9.3, should be thoroughly investigated, and the results analysed ideally by several people, to allow for possible different interpretations of the results.

The company itself

An in-depth analysis of the company itself is necessary, to show whether or not it is capable of entering certain fields, or whether others need to be expanded, or contracted.

The following areas should be considered.

1. Organisation
• What is the existing structure of the company?

- How are the different fields managed, i.e. is the work split into building, and civil engineering; or is it split by value, such as projects up to £200 000 and those over this figure?
- What is the communications network within the company? Both the formal and informal pathways should be investigated.
- What are the areas of operations, and the levels of resources in terms of skilled operatives, plant, supervisory personnel, stores facilities and specialist functions?

The results of this analysis should show whether the company can deal adequately with any new work, or whether major reorganising is necessary before new fields are entered, or workloads within existing fields are altered.

2. Management
- What is the experience and ability of the management?
- What is the outlook of management, is it very staid, or is it dynamic and enthusiastic?
- Will change be readily accepted or not? Too staid a management can lead to stagnation, whereas too enthusiastic a management could lead to overtrading in terms of finance and organisation, with bankruptcy as the outcome.

3. Trading records
These should be split up into the different fields of operation, and checked back over the previous years to determine the trends in the company's performance, with regard to overall profitability, capital employed, source of capital, profit as a percentage of capital employed, growth in turnover.

It is advantageous to compare the record of one's own company with those of similar companies engaged in similar work.

The results of these enquiries will show which are the most profitable areas of operations, and which require the most capital etc.

This section of the investigation is one of the most important, but is often the one that is carried out the most badly.

Materials sources

Types of materials can be classified as follows:

(a) Those that are generally problem free, with regard to quality, shortage in supply, or excessive price increases.
(b) Those prone to shortages in peak periods, such as bricks, cement, plaster and associated products. These are generally relatively low cost items compared to their bulk, where the manufacturers find it difficult to stockpile in times of industrial recession. This results in shortages, when the level of industrial activity is high.
(c) Those always having long delivery periods. This refers to such items as purpose-made components, steelwork etc. Many companies set up their own manufacturing units to produce joinery and concrete products, as these are then within the direct control of the parent company.

(d) Those prone to excessive price increases. Often these are due to actions beyond the control of industry or government, particularly where goods or raw materials are imported, such as copper from Zambia. These price increases may result from price increases at source, or from shortages.

The methods of acquisition of materials should be investigated, and will be from one of three types of source.

(a) Materials purchased from merchants. This is usually restricted to small items from manufacturers whose sales policy it is to operate through wholesalers only.

(b) Those materials purchased directly from the manufacturer. This often involves ordering in large quantities which may result in stockpiling being necessary.

(c) Materials purchased from within the company itself, e.g. aggregates from pits owned by the company, timber and joinery, precast concrete, bricks and blocks etc.

By analysing materials, degrees of risk and economies relating to materials can be investigated.

Market research

1. By client
Lists of details of the main clients within the different fields should be drawn up, including such details as:

- size of client's organisation
- value of potential contracts
- does the company deal with all clients in the market?
- has the company stopped dealing with particular clients, and if so, why?
- are the clients creditworthy?
- does each client generally deal only with one contractor for all its work, or many?
- how is the work placed; by package deal, or open tender etc?

2. By type of work
The potential work that is available in the different fields within an area should be investigated for as far into the future as possible. It would be pointless investing in specialist capital equipment that would not be fully utilised.

3. By competition
As much information as possible should be accumulated concerning the level of operations of competitors in each field, together with, if possible, details of their trading figures and organisation structure.

What is the company's share in each field of the market? Do the trends show an increasing or decreasing market share over the last few years?

4. Changes in consumer demand
Although this should have shown up in the market research, the volume of

certain types of construction work are often difficult to foresee, due to the type of work being in or out of favour with the consumers. High-rise development is a case in point. In the 1950s, tower blocks provided an answer to the problem of providing dwellings quickly, whilst at the same time taking up very little land. By the 1960s, it had become apparent that these were not the ideal choice of dwelling. Social problems developed, especially vandalism, and stability and maintenance problems were rife.

Today, very few companies would class high-rise housing as a possible growth market in the near future.

Research should also be carried out to determine what features customers require within their buildings.

Within offices, clients generally require an open-plan layout with demountable partitions and with suspended ceilings and access floors for ducting services to many outlets. These options allow rearrangement of layouts as the organisation or the leaseholders change.

When considering dwellings within particular geographical areas and price ranges the following factors might be important:

(a) number of bathrooms and bedrooms;
(b) fully fitted kitchen;
(c) double glazing and high thermal insulation;
(d) double garage;
(e) fully carpeted and curtained;
(f) landscaped garden.

5. The marketing mix

The marketing mix is dependent upon the analysis of points (1)−(4) above and leads to decisions which form the central core of the marketing policy. Within the marketing mix the four factors considered are:

- price − how much is to be charged;
- product − what is to be produced;
- place − where is it to be sold;
- promotions − what sales promotion techniques are used.

⎫
⎬ The 4 Ps
⎭

6. Sales promotion

Market research has to consider how best to promote the products made by the organisation.

The construction industry does not use many of the expensive advertising techniques used by other industries. Few construction companies advertise on TV for example. Unless the company is predominantly concerned with speculative development, there will not actually be a product to promote.

Some businesses promote services in which they specialise, e.g. glazing, thermal insulation, wall tiling, design and build for industry, etc. Most construction companies try to promote their good name, by keeping the company name or symbol in the public's eye. This can be done in many ways:

(a) Ensuring that there are clean site boundaries and entrances, with well-positioned signboards, and by inconveniencing the public as little as possible.

(b) Many companies adopt a symbol which is usually displayed alongside their name.
(c) The adoption of a company colour, with standard lettering or symbols on plant, lorries etc.
(d) Prestige buildings often have many large company nameboards, not only at the site entrance, but on tower cranes, scaffolding etc.
(e) Prestige buildings often have foundation or topping-out ceremonies, which are made much of in the local press.
(f) Good quality literature and stationery for the company can be well worth while, as this is often the first approach by the company to a client.
(g) When a company has a particularly interesting contract, a film unit may be commissioned to produce a film which can be shown later to prospective clients.

Again it is important to have a formal sales policy, with budgets for particular promotions. The return derived from money spent on advertising or other promotions is very difficult to assess, for a prospective client seeing a company advertisement today might not require their services for several years.

Analysis of relevant external influences

Many of the following examples cannot be foreseen with any degree of accuracy, but it must never be forgotten that these occurrences do happen, and accordingly contingency plans should always be built into any marketing strategy.

1. Government action
Due consideration must be given to the existing and future policies of government. For example:

- economic recession
- high interest rates
- lack of import controls
- low public expenditure all lead to a low level of construction work.

On the other hand the following could lead to a higher level of construction work:

- grants
- special development programmes such as airports, motorways, etc.
- export drives
- high public expenditure

2. Technology
Technological advances in construction methods and materials are constantly creating potential new markets for the building industry. For example, in the early 1960s, few people had heard about cavity-wall insulation. In the 1990s, there are now many businesses specialising solely in this work. Double glazing is yet another similar example of a booming industry, thanks to the soaring energy prices, which started in the early 1970s.

Plastics have revolutionised the industry, saving much labour on many sites. Manufacturers obviously saw great potential for the industry with such products as rainwater and drainage goods, septic tanks, window frames etc.

Failing wall ties in cavity walls have now led to a thriving industry using new techniques to replace old wall ties to make affected cavity walls structurally sound once again.

Companies must keep abreast of developments that may ultimately lead to increased demand from consumers.

3. Overseas governments

Political instability in the world can lead to fluctuations in the value of the pound. This may affect certain exporting companies, as a strong pound means that people abroad have to pay more for the goods that they are buying from this country. A drop in export sales could result in a cutting back in expansion programmes for exporting industries, which leads to less work for the construction industry.

Construction companies that are proposing to enter the overseas market must bear in mind the types of government that they will be dealing with. An appraisal of the country's past performance often helps to determine whether it is worth trying to carry out work there. For example the following points should be considered.

Is the country politically stable, or is it volatile, with frequent military takeovers?

Does the country in question enjoy good relations with Britain and the rest of the world?

Although this practice is tending to die out, in some countries in the past, giving gifts or inducements to certain officials was often the only way of securing work; this still persists to a small extent in some countries. In Britain this practice is illegal, but in some overseas countries it is tolerated. Should a company offer gifts or inducements to obtain work in such countries? If your answer is no, then the company may not obtain work there.

In this book, no attempt is made to make moral judgements, but merely to point out that when a company starts looking for work in overseas markets many different types of problems may occur.

- What level of inflation is there likely to be in the country, and what types of contract do they work to?
- Is the country wealthy, in its own right, or are contracts likely to be funded by western governments or world banking organisations?
- The attitude of local labour to construction work is important: are the workers lethargic, or energetic in their approach to work?
- Are there likely to be any problems from labour unions?

Following the analysis of the four areas under investigation, the marketing policy can be drawn up. This will include recommendations regarding the existing company, the materials sources and the markets.

The marketing policy should be constantly reviewed in all areas, using the targets set, through the feedback system.

Marketing management is said to consist of three elements:

Fig. 9.4 The formation and operation of a marketing policy

- analysis
- planning
- control

All three elements are included within the approach detailed within this chapter. The various areas of operations are analysed, detailed planning is then carried out based on the analysis and control is maintained by constantly measuring performance against targets. This can be seen by considering Fig. 9.4. This shows the feedback loops which indicate that change may be necessary to the policy in one of the four areas. The first area, that of the company structure and organisation, is the one most easily changed, as the company had direct control over it. The next group in which changes are most easily made is that of materials sources. Markets can be altered but often only slowly. The external influences generally cannot be affected at all by a single company. It is most important to remember that a marketing policy should be dynamic, and that it is not a once and for all operation.

Questions

1 Discuss the difficulties of marketing within the construction industry.
2 Within the construction industry, discuss the advantages of marketing, to the various parties concerned.
3 The construction industry spends relatively little on sales promotions, compared to some consumer good industries. Discuss reasons for this.

Chapter 10

Housing

Introduction

Types of housing stock

In December 1991 there were 23.6 million dwellings in the UK. Ownership of dwellings (given as a percentage) is now spread over four sectors:

	1981	1991
Owner occupied	55.8	67.6
Local authority & new town corporation	31.0	21.9
Private rented	11.2	7.3
Rented from housing association	2.1	3.1

Age of housing stock

The Building Regulations and before that the local Building Byelaws have developed and improved housing in the UK over the last few decades, particularly with regard to the internal environment concerning thermal insulation and moisture penetration. Much of the older housing stock still has problems of damp, with high heat loss through solid walls and uninsulated roofs. In 1991 the age distribution of dwellings (per cent) was as follows:

Pre-1891	14.0	1945–1970	32.1
1891–1918	12.6	post-1970	22.3
1919–1944	19.0		

The large percentage of older stock is one of the main reasons for the high level of maintenance work within the housing sector.

Building societies

By 1775 much of the common land in Britain had been enclosed and the agricultural revolution was just about to be replaced by the Industrial Revolution.

This change created a landless rural population of men and women who moved to towns looking for work. This led to two distinct classes, the working class, and the middle class, which earned its income from trade and commerce.

No welfare state existed at this time, and this led to mutual self-help in the working classes. Two examples are sick and burial clubs, and friendly societies. It was at this time that building societies began, indeed they are still administered today by the Chief Registrar of Friendly Societies. Men clubbed together and pooled their money in order to own their own houses. The earliest society was founded in 1775 in Birmingham, and within the next 50 years, at least 250 building societies were formed.

The usual plan was to use the accumulated savings to buy a plot of land and build houses on it. Each member would agree to pay the society a certain amount of money each month, until all the members were housed. The problem with this system was that it took many years to house all its members, and also that it was difficult to decide who should have the next completed house. The latter problem was often settled by pulling names out of a hat or by auction. When everyone was housed, the society was disbanded. About 1840 the long time periods that operated were reduced by the societies' borrowing from the wealthy middle classes, and giving interest on it. This necessitated charging interest on the money borrowed by the members. It was now realised that societies no longer needed to be terminated, but could be permanent, a name which still persists in the titles of many societies.

Various Acts were passed in 1874 and 1894 to help prevent frauds. By 1919 the assets of the societies were about £77 million, by 1939 this had increased 10 fold to £773 million. After the Second World War, there was a housing shortage, and mortgages had to be rationed. By 1945 the assets totalled £825 million but by 1950 this had grown to over £1200 million and in 1964 it was £4400 million.

From the beginning of this century, the number of societies has fallen, often due to amalgamations, from 2250 in 1900 to 900 in 1945 to 650 in 1964. Many of the earlier societies were terminating, so were due to close in any case.

The scene today is dominated by the large national building societies, but many smaller ones still exist. At the end of 1993 there were 83 societies with assets of £284 200 million. The amount lent on dwellings by building societies in 1993 was £31 511 million.

Today, societies borrow money from investors and offer interest, tax paid, to the investor. The interest offered will depend upon the length of time the money will be invested for, and whether regular monthly deposits are going to be made. The invested money is then lent out to people wishing to buy a new house or to extend an existing one. The interest paid is variable depending upon market forces, but is tax deductable up to a certain limit.

Housing Associations

In 1973 a white paper was put forward on housing, this talked of making housing associations the 'third arm' of housing, following owner occupied and private rented. This paper emphasised the importance of giving people a real choice between renting and owning. The 1974 Housing Act brought in by Labour consolidated the ideas of the 1973 white paper. Following the act there was much development of housing associations, mostly through the housing corporation but also by local authorities. The 1988 Housing Act has changed the financing of the associations. The National Federation of Housing Associations (NFHA) is the parent body to which over 2000 member associations are affiliated.

Housing associations are non-profit making, and their aim is to provide housing for people on low incomes or for those in housing need. They are organised and managed by voluntary individuals but medium and large associations employ professional staff. The management committee is responsible for formulating policy and ensuring that this is carried out.

The groups of people to whom the association rent can be very diversified and may include pensioners, single-parent families, disabled people, those with drink-related problems or the population in general.

Accommodation can be of either a permanent or a temporary nature. The properties offered might have been part of a new-build scheme or conversion of an old larger property into flats. In the past, housing associations generally rented property, but since the 1980 Housing Act they can now sell property.

Since 1989 housing associations have been encouraged to take over existing local authority estates, through the 'tenant's choice' provision of the 1988 Act.

In 1988 there were 2251 housing associations registered with the Housing Corporation. This is a government agency which develops and oversees the work of the member associations, and through which funds are channelled. Not all associations register with the Housing Corporation, but it is an advantage to do so if seeking public funds.

In 1989 500 000 homes were owned by housing associations, or 2.6 per cent of the housing stock. Since 1980 there have been dramatic cutbacks in local authority housing, with the government putting much more emphasis on housing provision through the housing associations. In 1988 the renting by housing associations to the different sectors was as shown in Fig. 10.1.

1980 Housing Act

The 1980 Housing Act gave a statutory right to nearly all council house tenants to buy their dwellings at a considerable discount. Certain properties were exempt, and the act has been updated. Here briefly are the main points of the scheme as it operates under the 1988 Housing Act.

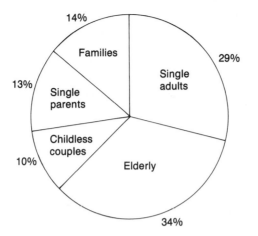

Fig. 10.1   Tenants of housing associations in 1988

(a) A tenant who has been in occupation for at least 2 years can obtain an initial discount of 32 per cent on a house, with an additional 1 per cent for every extra year of occupation, up to a maximum of 60 per cent. With a flat, the initial discount is 44 per cent, with an additional 2 per cent for every extra year of occupation up to a maximum of 70 per cent. This is subject to a maximum discount of £50 000.

(b) When the purchaser is unable to obtain a mortgage from normal sources, the local authority has to provide a 100 per cent mortgage subject to status.

(c) When the tenant desires to purchase the property, but has insufficient income to make the repayments, he can have the valuation price frozen for three years, on payment of a small refundable deposit. It is hoped that within the three years his income will have risen sufficiently to enable a loan to be obtained.

(d) After purchase the tenant must remain the owner for at least three years, otherwise a portion of the discount must be repaid.

The Act has resulted in the sale of some 1 400 000 dwellings between 1981 and 1991. This has inevitably led to a reduction in the local authority housing stock as very few replacements have been built to replace the sales due to restrictions placed on local authorities by the Conservative government.

The right to buy policy has led to the following:

(a) Local authorities have ever-extending housing waiting lists.

(b) Many tenants who bought their rented houses underestimated the costs of owning and maintaining a property. This was particularly so during periods of high interest rates. This has resulted in repossessions for some.

(c) One of the main reasons for the 'right to buy' policy was to relieve ratepayers and taxpayers of the burden of uneconomic local authority housing. In the past there have been many authorities who were not able to ask economic rents for properties, the shortfall in the housing revenue

132

budgets being made up from the general rate fund. It could be said that reducing the number of local authority properties for rent reduces the burden on society in general. At the same time the government is encouraging the development of housing associations where the tenants have much more say in the provision and management of the properties. Now, after the 1988 Housing Act, private funding is being encouraged.

The 1988 Housing Act

One of the principal objectives of this act was to encourage more private rented accommodation. It was hoped that by deregulating rent this could be brought about. As can be seen from Fig. 10.2 the private rented sector has diminished drastically since 1951. This could have been caused by:

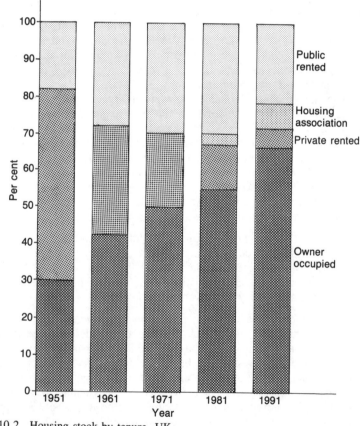

Fig. 10.2 Housing stock by tenure, UK
(*Source*: Housing and Construction Statistics)

(a) increased tenant's rights;
(b) landlords being at a tax disadvantage compared to owner occupiers;
(c) the high cost of administration and management of this sector.

The second important point covered by the act is that of 'tenant's choice'. This allows the tenants of local authorities and new town corporations to transfer to other landlords. In practice this has resulted in many local authority estates transferring their ownership to housing associations.

The third factor covered by the act is that of funding. Previously private funding was difficult to introduce into housing associations. The 1988 act, however, encourages part of the funding to come from the private sector, from building societies, banks or through share issue to the public.

The grant system has been changed, with housing association grants being reduced from figures of up to 100 per cent down to 75 per cent.

Factors affecting the erection and sale of housing

Demand for housing

The price of housing relative to incomes will undoubtedly affect what type of housing is sold or let. There is always a great demand for cheap housing, whether from local authority or housing association, because compared to other forms it is generally cheaper, this often only being accomplished at the expense of the ratepayer.

Where rented accommodation is not available, or is in very short supply, people have to think about becoming owner occupiers. Whether or not they buy houses is often determined by the cost and conditions of taking out a mortgage. Many large developers now operate their own mortgage schemes, thereby ensuring that buyers of their houses will not have great problems in acquiring a mortgage.

Certain jobs carry significant benefits when it comes to house purchase. Traditionally, employees of building societies and banks have been able to take out loans at much lower rates of interest than normal.

The demand for housing in a particular area is affected by the level of employment and the security of employment in that area. The south-east of England, for example, has house prices between 50 and 100 per cent higher than the rest of the country, for similar properties. This is a reflection of the need for accommodation in a relatively prosperous area, coupled with the problem of land shortage. Properties in South Wales, however, particularly in areas hit by heavy redundancies, for instance in the steel industry, are now selling for prices lower than if there were greater employment. This reflects the lack of demand, due either to people moving out of the area, or to a lower average income in the area.

During 1988 house prices peaked and then continued to drop until in 1993 in some areas of the UK house prices were only two thirds of the 1988 prices. There are several reasons for this:

(a) Until 1988 double tax relief was available on properties providing the man and woman who owned the property were not married. In 1988 before the double tax relief was removed there was a rush to buy before the cut-off date; this obviously fuelled the price rises.

(b) The economy and the housing market in particular was overheated in 1988 with many people taking on exceedingly large mortgages in order to buy properties before the cut-off date, as they thought prices would rise again, thus putting properties out of their reach.

(c) Since 1988 the economy has had a difficult period, with recession setting in, high unemployment and, due to exchange-rate difficulties, high interest rates until late 1992. These factors reduced people's confidence in the future, which in turn meant that people were less likely to commit themselves to large repayments on high mortgages. Less people wanted to move home, so the prices dropped.

Supply of housing

When the construction industry is working at peak capacity, the rate of completion of dwellings can be held up by non-availability of land, labour or materials. Land on which to build is becoming harder to find, and it is not unknown for large companies to employ land negotiators, whose job it is to seek out suitable parcels of land, often by air reconnaissance.

Labour and material shortages often occur, and are easily exacerbated by the government's stop−go policy. (See Chapter 19.)

The process of developing housing sites needs the availability of large amounts of money, which will not turn over quickly if houses stand unsold. Housing development is very sensitive to the level of interest rates. High rates can turn a potentially profitable site into a definite loss maker. One of the main determinants of housing availability is government policy. In the 1970s there were many suggestions and policy statements in government publications concerning housing policy.

It was suggested that there should be a fairly detailed though flexible national housing policy. This would be supplemented by local authorities preparing comprehensive local housing strategies (LHSs), which take into account the housing needs in a particular area. Coupled with these LHSs local authorities have to produce housing investment programmes (HIPs) covering their capital expenditure over a set period, normally four years. These HIPs are revised each year and central government will make capital spending allocations to each authority on the basis of these plans. It is hoped that by allowing local authorities to individually produce these plans, they will better cater for the particular housing needs within an area and will help make the local authorities more autonomous.

In the past, the criticism of unfairness has been levelled at government housing policy as local authority housing has been heavily subsidised by the central government and by local ratepayers. Owner occupiers have enjoyed very little in the way of subsidies. Current policy is tending to clear up this anomaly and to give people a fairer choice on their mode of occupation.

In order to encourage the growth of owner occupation, the government has in the past introduced a scheme whereby a first-time buyer can obtain a loan of £600 interest free for the first five years. The government policy to allow tax relief on mortgages up to a certain figure has also encouraged the growth of owner occupation.

The government has tried to control the use of land in various ways. Two such examples are:

(a) Development land tax (operating from 1976 until 1985), discouraged the sale of land for development, as a significant proportion of the increase in value was paid in tax. People often held on to the land in the hope of government eventually abolishing the tax, as has happened.

(b) The supply of suitable land is fixed to a certain extent by the various development plans of the local authority.

The effect of government policy is discussed in more detail in Chapter 19.

Land values and use

The value of land can be looked at from various viewpoints. Until the start of the twentieth century, the value of land was discussed mainly in *economic* terms, i.e. using the land to its greatest financial advantage.

Throughout history, and even today, land in many instances holds a significant *political* value. It may be that it is a strategic position for the military overseeing of a strip of nearby land or water. A particular piece of land may contain valuable mineral deposits, essential to the economy of a certain country.

In the last few decades, there has been an ever-increasing awareness of the *social* value of land. Playing fields and parks, for instance, hold a social value for the local community.

The *ecological* value of land is a subject which only in the last couple of decades has started to receive the attention required.

Economic value

The economic value of land is set by the demand for a particular plot, and this in turn is set by its location, climate, and environment, which gives rise to competition between the possible users. On purely economic grounds, the use that land is put to is based on deciding which alternative gives the greatest financial return within the time span considered. Land on the edge of a green belt, for instance, tends to be used for development rather than farming, providing, of course, planning permission is granted. For land gives a much lower return as farmland than it does as development land.

Development tends to have an irreversible mushrooming effect. For example, the decision to allow the building of a factory often leads to other factories, then houses, schools etc.

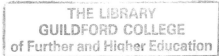

Town and Country Planning Acts, however, now ensure that land development is not the 'free for all' it was in the nineteenth century. Without town planning, the use of land would be unlimited, disorganised and very uneconomic.

The actual valuing of a plot of land is often fairly easy. One simply compares it with similar pieces recently valued or sold to arrive at a figure. If the land is to be sold, and an interest is shown by several people, it is often auctioned. There are sometimes situations when only one client is interested in purchasing; it is then necessary to try to determine the client's demand for the land. This may happen in the following situations, where it is often very difficult to arrive at a figure, as the value to this particular client may be many times the normal market value for the land.

(a) Part of a garden is sold to enable an access to be formed for an existing factory.
(b) Gardens of several houses are sold to a developer to form a viable building plot.
(c) One or two houses are sold and demolished, to allow access to land at the rear which can now be developed.

Social value

This could be defined as the value to the community, of a piece of land, in terms of health, well being, safety and general environment. Economic values as stated earlier are often fairly easy to fix quantitatively, whilst social values can only be discussed in qualitative terms, as described in Chapter 3.

Consider the following examples.

Example 1: A plot of land may be used for a library, a sports ground, or as a site for houses. As a library, it is a place for gaining enjoyment from literature; it aids society as a whole via education, possibly it even aids society economically. A sports ground provides a place for enjoyment, it also aids health which again could be said to aid society as a whole economically. Houses aid the community by providing accommodation.

Example 2: A plot of land is vacant in a town centre, what should it be used for?

Economically land is normally used for the purpose for which it is most suited, as the prospective users can each determine what utility it would hold for them. The client to whom it would give the greatest utility would normally pay the highest price, all things being equal.

A town centre position would economically dictate a use as shops, or offices, not houses or farmland. Social pressures may, however, require the provision of a library or police station.

A problem that often occurs is that what might at first seem a social benefit often ends up a social problem. For example, the repositioning of a heavy engineering factory to provide jobs may result in pollution in the form of smoke, dust, noise, traffic etc.

Government tries to set certain social values with the aid of legislation, such as the Town and Country Planning Acts, and various environmental health Acts. Encouragement is also given to the preservation of trees, historic buildings and monuments, and national parks.

Political value

The political value of land can be viewed from two standpoints:

(a) It may be politically advantageous to own or control a piece of land, for military reasons.
(b) In certain circumstances, government tries to encourage owners of land to use it in a particular way. This is done in order to benefit the country as a whole. For example:
   (i) During the Second World War, the 'dig for victory' campaign encouraged people towards self-sufficiency.
   (ii) In the 1930s, food subsidies were given to farmers to encourage them to grow sugar beet and wheat for self-sufficiency.
   (iii) In development areas, the government tries to help the setting up of new industries by offering grants. This is often to try to relieve an unemployment problem.
   (iv) In the national interest, government may sanction the working of open-cast coal mines in a farming area. Here conflict arises between the social value of beautiful countryside and the economic value to the country of coal reserves.

Ecological value

This is really concerned with factors which affect the continuation of various forms of life. A few examples are as follows:

(a) Pollution of rivers by industrial effluent is likely to kill off fish stocks.
(b) Urbanisation in general leads to the destruction of many natural habitats of fauna and flora.
(c) The destruction of hedgerows by farmers to produce larger more easily worked fields again destroys natural areas so often used for nesting.
(d) The increase of agricultural output by the use of pesticides has led to the decline of many bird populations.

In nearly all the above situations, a conflict arises between the ecological and the economic value of land.

Who benefits from the use of land?

When considering land value, it is very seldom one person who derives the benefit from a particular use. Consider the following. Many people derive a benefit from a high-street shop in a town centre:

- The owner obtains an income.
- The employees obtain an income.
- The customers obtain satisfaction for their needs.
- Suppliers of goods and services to the shop are kept in employment.

In general town centres are used for the benefit of society, whereas suburbs and farmland tend to give greater benefit to the individual.

Questions

1 Why is there still a need for housing associations in modern society?
2 Should local authorities be forced to sell their dwelling units to tenants?
3 In the past there has been talk by certain governments of nationalising land. If such a measure ever did come into effect, what would be the advantages and disadvantages?
4 In your opinion, should there be more rented or more privately owned housing, and why?

Chapter 11

Production equilibrium of the firm

Introduction

When studying the action of any production unit, it is necessary to take into account the type of competition likely to be met in the market in question. In the eyes of the economist, competition can exist anywhere between two extremes. These extremes are known as perfect competition and perfect monopoly. Like the concept of planned and free economies discussed earlier, they are unreal situations which are only assumed, to try to simplify interactions into simple processes that economists can use to interpret the actions of real situations. See Fig. 11.1.

Fig. 11.1 Types of competition

Perfect competition

Perfect competition is a concept much used by economists, to study the effect on production and consumption of the action of supply and demand. The conditions necessary for perfect competition were detailed in Chapter 5, but to reiterate, they were:

(a) All products are homogeneous.
(b) A large number of buyers and sellers.
(c) There is perfect market knowledge.
(d) All factors of production are perfectly mobile.
(e) All commodities produced are perfectly mobile.
(f) All firms are free to enter or leave the industry.

Perfect monopoly

For perfect monopoly to exist, there are two conditions to be met.

(a) There must be no substitute for the particular commodity. This is usually the more difficult of the two conditions to comply with, as nearly all commodities have alternatives.
(b) There is only one producer.

Under perfect monopoly, the supplier has complete control over the supply of goods, and may choose to do one of two things: (a) He may fix the quantity of goods that will be produced. In this case the customers will fix the price. (See Fig. 11.2(a).) (b) Alternatively, the supplier may decide to fix the price at which the goods will be sold. This leaves the consumers free to choose what quantity will be demanded at that price. (See Fig. 11.2(b).)

Imperfect competition

In a real situation, imperfect competition exists, because:

(a) There is very little mobility of the factors of production.
(b) Products produced by modern industry are not identical, each have small differences, if only in brand name, which in itself can imply good or mediocre quality in the eyes of the consumer.
(c) It is not all that easy for firms to enter or leave an industry, particularly if that industry is highly capital intensive. It is not always possible to quickly convert machinery and other capital items such as specialist buildings into cash with which to purchase the capital items necessary for operation within

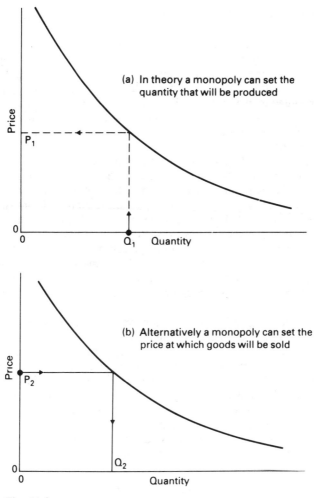

(a) In theory a monopoly can set the quantity that will be produced

(b) Alternatively a monopoly can set the price at which goods will be sold

Fig. 11.2

another industry. Industry in real life has to take a much longer-term view than that implicit in the theory of perfect competition.

Although one hears much talk of a monopoly existing within certain industries, this would not be a perfect monopoly which complied with the two criteria stated earlier.

For example, British Rail may be thought to have a monopoly of rail transport, but again there are small independent railway companies, and there are always alternatives to rail transport.

It is this problem of there always being alternatives, that generally prevents perfect monopoly from existing.

As can be seen from Fig. 11.1, imperfect competition can exist anywhere between the two extremes.

A type of competition operating very close to perfect monopoly is oligopoly. Here, there are only very few suppliers, and each commands a significant market share. As there are so few suppliers, if one reduces prices, then the others have to follow in order not to lose sales. It is because of this potential price-war situation that price fixing, or the forming of cartels, is often attempted. In these circumstances, competition for sales is concentrated not on price, but on such things as advertising, the benefits of after sales service, or even free gifts.

Another type of imperfect competition is monopolistic competition. This occurs very often in modern trading, and is where there are large numbers of manufacturers whose products are close, but not perfect, substitutes.

For example, many manufacturers produce cars, but there is only one Rolls Royce. Other cars could be classed as an alternative means of transport, but if a person specifically wanted a Rolls Royce, then there is no substitute.

Similarly, a coffee-processing firm might sell its coffee under the name of 'Brown bean'. As this would be a registered trademark, this company would have the monopoly of selling Brown bean coffee. Again there is no substitute for the real Brown bean, but there are many substitutes within the market for coffee.

Monopolistic competition is close to perfect competition, except that the products are not homogeneous, but individual.

In the UK there is much legislation concerning monopolies and restrictive practices. The Monopolies and Restrictive Practices Act 1948 caused the formation of the Monopolies and Mergers Commission. Under the present law, a supplier is defined as being in a position of monopoly if he holds 25 per cent or more of the market. This legal definition of monopoly must not be confused with the economic definition.

Since 1948, many Acts have been passed to try to encourage freer competition and better service in the public interest. Some of the relevant Acts are listed below:

- The Restrictive Trade Practices Act 1956
- The Fair Trading Act 1973
- The Restrictive Trade Practices Act 1976
- The Resale Prices Act 1964 and 1976

Returns to scale

In this chapter are discussed the various criteria which affect the attaining of the optimum production enterprise. The external influence of competition has been investigated, the internal problems of the scale of operations will now be considered.

In Chapter 1, the law of diminishing returns was demonstrated. Broadly speaking, this was defined as the effect of adjusting a variable factor, or factors, in combination with one or more fixed factors. The term 'returns to scale' refers to the outcome of varying all the factors of production, to cater for increased production requirements.

If, for instance, all the factors were increased by 50 per cent but the output increased by only 40 per cent, then this would be an example of decreasing returns to scale. If, on the other hand, the output increased by 50 per cent, then this would represent constant returns to scale. If, however, a 50 per cent increase in all factors resulted in a 60 per cent increase in output, then this would show increasing returns to scale. This last example is the most common of the three, and is related to the advantages of economies of scale discussed in Chapter 12.

At this point, this effect of varying the factors will be analysed more fully. The object of trying to determine the optimum criteria is, so that within any particular time period, the maximum returns can be obtained for the minimum cost, which is another way of saying that the profit is maximised.

The costs borne by a producer can be divided into two types:

1. Fixed costs. These are those that do not vary in the short term. In a typical manufacturing business these would be represented by the buildings, large machinery, the management itself, etc., in other words the items that could not be changed quickly. Over a wide range of output, it can be seen that the fixed costs can remain constant.

2. Variable costs. These are those that vary with the amount of output. In a typical producing business, this would be represented by raw materials, labour costs, energy costs in using the machines etc.

From a study of the nature of a firm's costs, the short term or short period can be defined as the period of time in which a firm's fixed costs remain constant.

Similarly the long term, or long run, or long period, can be defined as any length of time greater than that in which it takes to change fixed costs.

The definition of short and long period is therfore likely to be different for various industries, as their costs are built up differently.

The following can be deduced:

total costs = fixed costs + variable costs

Production equilibrium

This takes into account the fixed and variable costs, and can best be seen using an example as follows.

A small joinery manufacturer, specialising in the production of timber staircases, has the following cost figures, as in Table 11.1. These figures can be interpreted into graph form, as on Figs. 11.3–11.5.

Table 11.1 Output costs of staircase manufacture

Output/day (staircases)	Fixed cost (£)	Average fixed cost per unit (£)	Variable cost (£)	Average variable cost per unit (£)	Total output cost (£)	Marginal cost (£)		Average total cost per unit (£)
0	100	—	0	—	100			—
1	100	100	80	80	180	80	75	180
2	100	50	150	75	250	70	67.5	125
3	100	33.3	215	71.7	315	65	65	105
4	100	25	280	70	380	65	72.5	95
5	100	20	360	72	460	80	95	92
6	100	16.7	470	78.3	570	110	137.5	95
7	100	14.3	635	90.7	735	165	195	105
8	100	12.5	860	107.5	960	225	262.5	120
9	100	11.1	1 160	128.9	1 260	300		140

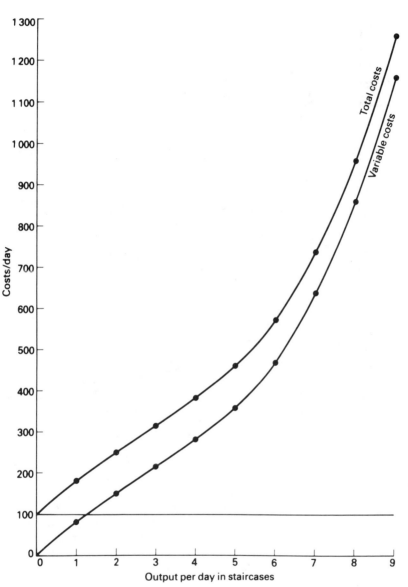

Fig. 11.3   Fixed and variable costs

On Fig. 11.3, it can be seen that the fixed costs remain constant over the whole range of outputs considered here. If it was decided to expand output to say 20 or 30 units per day, it would probably be necessary to increase the fixed costs involved. If this were not done, then the law of diminishing marginal returns would set in.

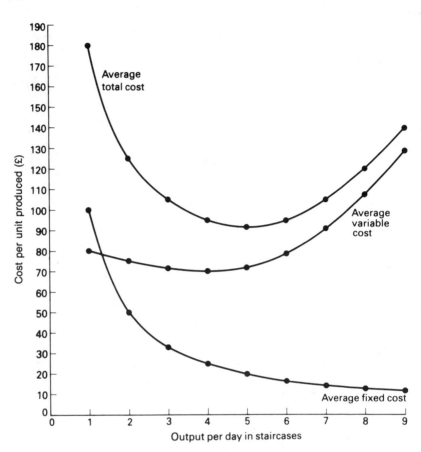

Fig. 11.4 Average production costs per unit

Figure 11.4 shows the relationship between the average variable cost and average total cost. Looking at the average fixed costs line, it can be seen that the more goods that are produced from an enterprise with a certain mix of fixed costs, the lower will be the fixed cost commitment per unit.

Variable costs on the other hand can be seen to drop, up to a certain level of output, then rise steeply again, this demonstrating yet again the law of diminishing returns.

The average total cost is the addition of the two lower lines, and this too follows in general the pattern of decreasing to a certain level of output, then increasing again.

Figure 11.5 compares the average total cost with the marginal cost. Marginal cost is defined as the incremental cost involved in producing one more unit of output in a given period. Conversely, a marginal return or marginal revenue is the incremental return obtained from the sale of one more unit of output in a given period.

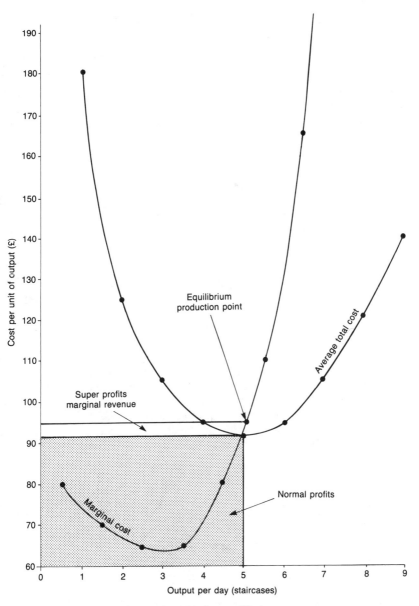

Fig. 11.5 The determination of production equilibrium

To be able to determine the production equilibrium point, which is the optimum level for production, it is necessary to investigate the returns from sales. Consider Table 11.2, and Fig. 11.5.

As can be seen in Fig. 11.5, after a certain point the marginal costs of

Table 11.2   Revenue and profitability of sales of staircases

Output/day (staircase)	Total revenue (£)	Marginal revenue* (£)	Total costs (£)	Marginal cost (£)	Profit (£)
0	—	—	100	—	−100
1	95	95	180	75	−85
2	190	95	250	67.5	−60
3	285	95	315	65	−30
4	380	95	380	72.5	0
5	475	95	460	95	15
6	570	95	570	137.5	0
7	665	95	735	195	−70
8	760	95	960	262.5	−200
9	855	95	1260	—	−405

* Marginal revenue is constant

production increase. It is, however, most profitable for the business if production is increased as long as the marginal cost of producing the last unit of output is less than the marginal return.

The maximum profit equilibrium point is attained where marginal cost equals marginal revenue.

If a business is operating below this output, then it will be more profitable to increase output. If the marginal cost is higher than the marginal revenue, then obviously it will be more profitable to reduce output. This can be seen from Table 11.2; the greatest profit is made where the marginal cost equals the marginal revenue with an output of five units per day. In this particular case, if the output is varied up or down by one unit, then there is zero profit.

Over the long term, the marginal return must at least equal the average total cost. If this were not the case, then the enterprise would have to go out of business. If many firms were in this state, because of a recession, then below normal profits would be made which would induce firms to leave the industry. This is shown on Fig. 11.6 at position E_2. If on the other hand large super profits were being made as at position E_3 of Fig. 11.6, then many firms might enter the industry. When only normal profit is made, then firms neither join nor leave the industry, and the industry is said to be in a state of equilibrium.

If a firm is operating at a point where only normal profits were made, then the firm is said to be operating at a long-term equilibrium point. See Fig. 11.6, point E_1. If it is operating so that either below or above average profits are made, then assuming the theory of perfect competition, changes occur. The firm in these circumstances is said to be operating at a short-term equilibrium point.

Fig. 11.6 Short- and long-term equilibrium positions

Linear programming

After following through the previous example, based on fixed and variable costs, and the revenue obtained, it is possible to determine the equilibrium production point for the particular circumstances existing within the firm at that time. If a detailed analysis is going to be carried out on the firm's production, how is it possible to determine the correct mix of factors that might enter into such an analysis?

One such method now being widely used, is that of linear programming. This is an analytical approach used by many organisations to either maximise profit or, in the case of non-profit-making bodies, minimise costs. Using this method, the available resources, systems and marketing constraints are expressed in the form of mathematical equations and inequalities. These are then solved, often with the aid of computers, for any given set of input figures. By using this system, the optimum values can be determined for inputs and other requirements.

This type of analysis is frequently used for determining such things as maintaining an efficient bus service, or milk delivery service.

In the context of building, it could be used with reference to a precast concrete workshop, or mass-produced joinery factory, to determine the optimum working system for given inputs or required outputs. When applied to such a situation, it could show the best flow path, physical layout, machine times, stock levels etc. on the different flow paths available, by feeding in the required output needed, together with the input equations.

A detailed examination of linear programming is beyond the scope of this book, but the student should bear the process in mind, for it could be used much more in the future, with the increasing use of microcomputers.

Questions

1 Discuss the difference between perfect competition and perfect monopoly.
2 (a) Determine the production equilibrium point for the staircase manufacturer discussed earlier, given the following information.

Selling price £145.
Fixed costs £90 per day.

Variable costs/day	110	210	300	400	530	680	860
Output/day	1	2	3	4	5	6	7

(b) What profit is made at this point?
3 Discuss why a firm can not exist at a short-term equilibrium point for a long period, assuming perfect competition is in operation.

Chapter 12

The scale of production

Introduction

If the type of business enterprises existing today is compared with those of 50–100 years ago, it will be seen that there are many more larger businesses today than in years gone by. One important reason for the growth of larger companies is the advances made in communications at all levels over the last few decades. In particular, with reference to telecommunications, postal services, transport, and data distribution systems in general. These have enabled faster distribution of goods and information, from a few large national production units, rather than from many smaller locally based industries. This has led to firms operating not only on a national level, but often multinationally.

Why, one may ask, do firms grow to such large sizes, for there must be reasons other than communications?

The main reason for the existence of a business is to make a profit, and very often, the larger the firm, the greater the profit, due to economies of scale.

Economies of scale

These may be classified either as internal or external economies of scale.

Internal economies of scale

These are economies that arise from within the firm itself. They can be described as follows.

1. Bulk purchase of raw materials. The larger the production operation, the more raw material will be required. This generally enables the firm to obtain bulk supplies at a reduced cost. By moving from purchasing on a small scale to purchasing on a large scale, very often the firm can bypass the middleman or wholesaler. This is particularly so in the construction industry, where, for example, a small company might buy cement or bricks in small lots from a builders' merchant, whereas a large company would have large direct loads which are despatched straight from the factory, at a much lower cost per unit.

2. Bulk sales. On increasing production, a firm needs to sell more goods. Again, favourable rates can often be obtained for selling large lots rather than small. A typical example is where an estate agent might normally require 2 per cent commission on the sale of a few houses erected by a developer. With a site of 100 houses, however, the same agent might agree to sell the houses for 1 per cent commission.

3. Division of labour. The larger the firm, the greater the opportunity to carry out division of labour, with all its associated advantages, as discussed in Chapter 4. Greater output should inevitably lead to the more economical use of plant. This is because the more work there is available, the less likelihood of the plant lying idle.

4. Borrowing money. It is often said that large firms have a better facility for the borrowing of money, as the larger the firm, the more stable and secure it seems in the eyes of an investor. The actual cost of borrowing large amounts of money is, however, often higher than that of borrowing smaller amounts.

5. Research and development. A large company can afford to employ specialists, and carry out detailed research, which would not be financially possible for a smaller firm. This often results in large firms remaining market leaders, as they maintain a flow of technological developments which enables them to stay ahead of their competitors.

6. Administrative economies. Large-scale production often leads to economies in administration. For instance, if a manufacturing firm doubled its turnover, it is unlikely that the numbers of managers and clerks employed would be doubled.

7. Improved benefits. Large firms often provide much better social facilities and fringe benefits than could be offered by smaller companies. This has the benefit of improving working conditions and reducing the turnover of staff.

External economies of scale

A firm may gain benefit by virtue of the industrial environment within a location, rather than from any internal changes in the firm. Such points to consider might be:

1. Existing service industries. When there is a large multi-industry population within an area, many service industries will already exist to service a wide range of industries. For example, transport facilities, banking and insurance facilities, suppliers and wholesalers of all materials, electric motor rewinders etc.

2. Specialist industries. When a similar industry exists on a large scale within a region, the operation of division of labour will often have created specialist firms, which can carry out certain types of work cheaper than a large multipurpose firm.

A good example is a typical industrial area in the Midlands. Here engineering work of all types is carried out, and has led to many specialist firms, e.g: pattern makers; toolmakers; chromium platers; galvanisers; specialist waste disposal firms.

3. Local labour and training. If a firm is thinking of entering an area in which the industry already exists, then there is likely to be an existing supply of labour trained in the particular skills required. Should labour have to be trained, however, then there often exists good training facilities locally for the skills required.

The optimum size of firms

Firms engaged in different types of industries require different sizes of production unit for optimum efficiency. Consider the following:

(a) A blacksmith will operate best when he is self-employed with possibly a couple of staff to assist. In other words a very small-scale operation.
(b) The manufacture of motor cars needs a production unit on a vast scale, if it is to achieve the economies of scale necessary to make a profit.

Although earlier it was stated that firms grow in order to made greater profits, some firms are more profitable on a small scale by virtue of the type of work they do. Some reasons why certain businesses stay fairly small follow.

1. Specialists providing personal attention. Work requiring the personal attention of a specialist. Architects, for example, are nearly always to be found in fairly small practices, as their personal attention is required by the client.

Once a private architect's practice grows to a certain size, it is difficult to maintain the personal contact, and much more time is spent by the senior partners in supervising and correcting the mistakes or inadequacies of the other employees. This example demonstrates a fairly low threshold for the setting in of diseconomies of scale.

2. Small specialist businesses. Within a particular geographical region, there is sometimes only enough work for one or two small business units of a particular type, e.g. tree surgeons. As there is normally so little demand for a tree surgeon within any particular area, if the firm tried to expand, a great deal more travelling would have to be done in order to obtain work. This would increase costs, and so again diseconomies of scale begin.

3. Specialist craft businesses. Where particular craft skills are required, for example in the production of hand-made goods such as woodcarving, decorative plasterwork or stained-glass windows, it is very difficult to employ extra labour and therefore expand, as there are so few people with the exceptional skills that would be required.

As was seen in Chapter 7, there are very many small firms within the construction industry who cater mainly for the repair, maintenance and specialist subcontract market.

When there are no constraints keeping the optimum size small, then firms may grow in different ways.

Expansion of the existing operation

A firm may increase its turnover by carrying out more of the same sort of work that has been handled in the past, and this is the most common form of growth. For instance, a contracting firm may decide to carry out more or larger contracts than in the past. It is hoped that this will lead to greater profits.

Combination

Here a firm will either take over, or amalgamate with, another or others, to form a single more efficient unit. Combination can take place in two forms:

1. Horizontal combination. This is where a firm will join with another firm that is carrying out similar business. For example a building firm may decide to take over another building firm in the same area for various reasons. It may be that the two firms are in fierce competition with one another, and so getting rid of this competition may lead to increased profit margins. Another reason for this merger may be that the firm being taken over holds considerable land banks that would be useful to a building development company.

2. Vertical combination. This is where firms combine, so that the different levels of the production and possibly distribution of a product are brought under common ownership.

For example a building company might take over a builders' merchant, so that in times of materials shortages, the building company will have security of supply. This would be a downwards combination, as the building company would be combining down the production chain.

Alternatively, a speculative development company may take over an estate agents, in order to hold power in the selling of their properties, and to enjoy the benefits of associated building society backing, which is often allied to estate agents' work. This particular type of merger is known as an upward combination, as the builder is combining up the production chain.

In order for company A to take over company B, it is necessary for company

A to obtain 51 per cent of the voting shares (a majority holding) of company B. Company A is then known as a holding company with full control over company B. By this method of takeover, very large groups or combines of businesses are possible.

The growth of multinational companies

In the last 20 years, there has been considerable growth in the size of many companies, to the extent that their area of operations now covers several countries. There are several possible reasons that might persuade a company to expand in this manner.

(a) Many businesses try to combine vertically to take under their control raw material supplies that have to be imported. A good example of this is the possession by tea and rubber firms operating in Britain of extensive plantations abroad. By this means, they can ensure that the raw materials are not sold to competitors.

(b) In order to improve sales and widen the market for its goods, a company may set up an operation in another country, to sell goods. This can take many different forms. For instance, American oil companies set up subsidiary companies in Britain, in order to sell their petrol to British motorists.

In some instances, to overcome restrictions on the importing of finished products, it is necessary to build an assembly plant in the country in question in order to be able to bring the goods in, in component form, assemble them into finished goods and sell them. For example, several Japanese car manufacturers have set up production plants in the UK in order to have access to the European market.

(c) In the past, many companies have developed manufacturing and assembly plants in countries either where labour costs were low, or where there was little disruption to production caused by strikes etc. This helps to ensure that costs are kept low, and that production targets will be met.

(d) Very often, when there is high unemployment in a particular region of a country, the government will offer financial assistance, in the form of grants, to encourge foreign firms to set up businesses there.

(e) When a company has many production units in many countries, the purpose is frequently to offset the problem of recession that might occur in any one particular country. This spreads the risks of the total enterprise over as wide a base as possible.

(f) In some countries, there is a very low rate of 'corporation' tax. This encourages companies to carry out business in these countries, for this could lead either to higher direct profit margins, or to lower productive costs which in turn should lead to higher demand and eventually to more profits.

Input—output analysis

In the study of the economy of the firms of a particular country, it is necessary to try to collate the information concerning the various inputs and outputs of the different industries, to see how all industries relate to one another. The study of such interactions can be carried out with the aid of an input—output table.

An input—output table is a matrix in which the various producers and consumers are each allocated a row and a column within the table. The inputs and outputs of these producers and consumers, can then be analysed.

Consider Table 12.1. The total output from manufacturer A is £1 200 000 worth of goods, of which £800 000 worth goes to other manufacturers, £200 000 worth to the home consumers, and £200 000 worth is exported. The value of inputs into manufacturer A balances the output, with £800 000 coming from other manufacturers, £300 000 being the value of labour, profits and taxes, and £100 000 worth of goods coming in directly as imports. By studying the table, it can be seen to what extent each industry is dependent upon another.

Likely repercussions of possible actions can easily be seen. For example:

(a) If the government decided to restrict the sale of exports to 50 per cent of the existing (not a very likely action in practice), then manufacturer D would lose £600 000 of sales immediately, and would have to try and sell more in the home market.

(b) If government policy were to restrict imports, then again manufacturer D might be hard hit, as this firm uses a large proportion of imported inputs.

(c) From the table, it can be seen that manufacturer A supplies £500 000 of goods to manufacturer B. If A went out of business, then B might be in serious difficulties, as $\frac{5}{8}$ of its inputs come from A.

Table 12.1 An example of a simple input output table (figures are in £100 000)

	Manufacturer					Inter-mediate output	Home market	Export market	Final output	Total output
	A	B	C	D	E					
Manufacturer A	—	5	1	0	2	8	2	2	4	12
Manufacturer B	1	—	0	3	1	5	4	2	6	11
Manufacturer C	4	1	—	0	0	5	1	0	1	6
Manufacturer D	1	0	3	—	5	9	0	12	12	21
Manufacturer E	2	2	0	0	—	4	10	0	10	14
Inputs other than goods and services	3	3	2	12	4	24	—	—	—	24
Imports	1	0	0	6	2	9	10	—	10	19
Total inputs	12	11	6	21	14	64	27	16	43	107

From Table 12.1 which, it must be stressed, is a very simple example, the ratio of imports to exports can also be deduced.

Very complex tables can be drawn up, to show the inter-relationship of all industries, services, consumer sectors etc. within a country. By doing this, it is much easier to study situations than by wading through masses of figures in statistical lists.

Questions

1 The optimum size for a building firm is large. Discuss this statement.
2 What could be shown by considering input–output analysis applied to the construction industry, its suppliers and customers?
3 Why is it so much more difficult to obtain economies of scale within the construction industry compared to a car production factory?

Chapter 13

The location of industry

Introduction

In the past there were many factors influencing the location of industry. Today, in developed societies, some of these factors are now less important, thanks to the developments in education, transport, communications and power supplies, as will be seen.

A firm needs to operate at its most efficient level; if it does not, its competitors will be able to undercut its prices and eventually the firm will go out of business. By carefully locating the place of business, certain costs can be minimised. The following six factors may need to be considered.

Location factors

Nearness of power supply

In the industrial revolution, with the beginning and growth of industry, it was essential to have a nearby source of power. This was one of the main reasons for the development of the woollen industry in Yorkshire. Here were ample streams which would provide power for the looms and other machinery, with the aid of waterwheels. Later on, with the advent of steam power, it became important for industries to be centred on or near coal producing areas. Hence the reason for the positioning of many power requiring industries in the Midlands, South Wales and around Manchester.

With the coming of the twentieth century, other forms of power were being developed, so that with the completion of supply networks for electricity and gas, and with oil being fairly easy to transport, the location for reasons of power supply is no longer so critical in many cases.

Coal, when required in large amounts, is still a very important factor, for due to its bulk, it is very expensive to transport. It is for this reason that electricity power stations designed for burning coal are still constructed close to coal mines, to cut down transport costs.

Nearness of raw materials

The transporting of any raw material involves costs which vary with the distance, unless there is a set price delivered anywhere in the country, or within certain regions. The price of cement for instance would be the same in many areas, for the price is fixed nationally, to a certain extent. It is obvious that transport distances should be cut wherever possible in order to cut costs. This is especially important with low-cost, high-bulk materials. These are said to only have a high value close to their place of origin, and so are termed high place-value materials. Examples of these would be sand and gravel used for roadworks and concrete, and clay for brickmaking. A businessman wishing to set up a production plant for precast concrete, or brick manufacture, would be extremely foolish if the site chosen were not close to good raw material sources.

As the cost of oil rises, so do transport costs. In the future, when transport costs could form a much larger proportion of the selling price of an article, the nearness to raw materials could be even more important than it is today.

Nearness to a market

Certain types of goods have to be near to potential markets; again these are goods which are heavy to transport. As in the last section, precast concrete products and bricks fall into this category. It can be seen already that when locating an enterprise there is often a compromise between nearness to raw materials and nearness to markets. A factory that had to transport its products over long distances would be at a price disadvantage compared to a competitor who only transported a short distance. Where breakable goods are being transported, long hauls can often be very expensive if many breakages occur.

Other goods, which tend to be fairly scarce, and where transport costs only form a small percentage of total cost, for example motor cars or televisions, do not need to be too close to markets. Indeed, at the present time, Japan is selling both these commodities to Britain.

Pilfering is a major problem that must be borne in mind, when transporting high-cost, scarce goods, over long distances.

High future transport costs could again make the nearness to markets another more important factor in the future.

Transport and communication

Closeness to transport is always very important. In Britain, many industrial centres developed around the networks of canals and railways in the eighteenth and nineteenth centuries. With the advent of a good road system, all markets now become easily attainable.

When transport is a major factor, however, especially when hauling heavy materials, then a considerable financial advantage can be gained over competitors by siting the production plant close to a motorway junction, or in certain circumstances a separate rail link may be run to the factory.

In some cases new transport systems have led to the development of new business or commercial centres. This is particularly true in the case of the M25, which has caused a relative increase in office rents outside London, compared to the city centre. The retail development at Lakeside Thurrock is another example of commerce following the M25.

At present, thanks to relatively cheap transport, many industries can afford to have one, or only a few, production centres, and can transport the goods all over the country. As transport gets relatively more expensive, will the economic market area for industries become smaller? This may lead to regional markets where national ones now exist, or local markets where regional ones now exist.

The external economies of scale

These were discussed in the last chapter, and they all help to form a decision as to the ideal location for an industry. One point is particularly important, however, and that is the closeness of a suitable source of labour, and specialist suppliers. If skilled and trained labour already exist in an area then much time and money could be saved through not having to train operatives.

As was mentioned in Chapter 2, labour tends to be very immobile and so it is difficult to attract trained labour to an area. This is yet another reason for establishing an enterprise in an area where a pool of labour exists.

The intervention of government

(See also social problems and attitudes in Chapter 4.) Over the last few decades, there has been a decline in certain industries, particularly those associated with the North of England, such as shipbuilding and the textile industries. The new technology industries, however, have tended to concentrate in the Midlands and the South East. This has led to an imbalance of industrial activity within the different regions of the country.

The various governments since the 1930s have tried to overcome this problem by the granting of certain types of aid to those areas needing assistance. There are at present three types of assisted area:

(a) special development areas, where the needs are most urgent
(b) development areas, where the needs are less severe
(c) intermediate areas, where some help is needed, but not urgently

Regional development grants for machinery and buildings in specified manufacturing industries are made under the 1972 Industry Act, whilst other grants are available, providing they aid employment in an assisted area.

Government also helps these areas in two other ways:

(a) Firms in assisted areas get preferential treatment when tendering for government contracts.
(b) Government is keen to give fast approval to industrial development certificates (IDC) in assisted areas. Approval for an IDC in a non-assisted area generally takes a little longer.

Since joining the EEC, areas of Britain suffering industrial change or severe unemployment are eligible for grants from the European Regional Development Fund.

The development of rural industries and small firms is carried out through the Council for Small Industries in Rural Areas (CoSIRA). Technical and managerial advice is given, and loans and credit facilities are arranged. This has helped develop many small businesses in areas where there was previously little chance of increasing employment.

The previous six factors are those particularly relevant to many industries in Britain today. In Britain in the past, and indeed in other less developed countries today, different factors often have to be taken into account.

The stability of the political situation

Businessmen, wishing to develop a production unit in countries abroad, look very seriously at this problem. When the political climate is volatile, with much unrest, production from industries within this type of environment can be seriously disrupted, as can transport facilities. There are also many situations where governments have compulsorily nationalised foreign investments, sometimes without compensation.

Climate

This was very important for certain industries in the past. A good example of this is the production of woollen cloth in Lancashire and Yorkshire, where the correct degree of humidity existed for the processing of the fibres.

Today, climatic problems are only really considered a problem in the food and other organic industries, such as the growing of cotton or rubber trees etc. Manufacturing is not now so affected by extremes or wrong types of climate, for thanks to technology, almost any type of climate can be created artificially using air-conditioning techniques.

Proximity to main centres of commerce etc.

It is often a great advantage to have a business operation close to centres of commerce, finance and government. Close links can be formed with other types of commerce, and large contracts can often be won, purely because of public relations exercises, or by personal contact which is possible when many industries are grouped together.

Many large industries operate a branch office, if not the head office, from London, purely because it is the centre of commerce and government, and because much trade is negotiated there.

The speed and efficiency of modern modes of passenger transport, however, means that two business meetings, which took place at opposite ends of the country, could be managed in the same day.

How the location factors affect different industries

In Table 13.1, the letters A, B, C, have been used to try to give some indication of the importance of a particular location factor to each industry considered, A being the most important, C the least.

Some of the table is left blank, and as an exercise, after reading this section, the student should fill in the spaces, and discuss his choice of weightings.

As power is so well distributed in this country, the positioning of an industry close to power is no longer so critical here. The table, however, tries to give some idea of the importance of power to the industry, as this is still often considered in overseas locations.

Car industry

Here much power is used in total, from the pressings and castings of the manufacture of components, to the assembling and finishing processes.

The car industry can be defined at different levels of operation.

It is possible to talk of the car industry as virtually an assembly and finishing process, or one could include all the preliminary basic manufacture of components. The latter example is the one favoured here, and, as so much steel is used in the production of cars, it is fairly important to have good local sources of supply in sheet and other form.

A close market is not nowadays all that important, for cars are shipped between many countries of the world, and as the cost of transporting cars within a country bears an insignificant part of the total cost (about 1−2 per cent of the selling price), other factors are more important.

The closeness of specialised suppliers to the car industry is very important. Within the industry, components for just one type of car are often manufactured by hundreds of different suppliers. An ideal situation then would be to position a car assembly plant within close proximity to these suppliers. Specialist service industries, such as machinery manufacturers, should also be close at hand.

A car assembly plant, complete with machinery, costs many millions of pounds, therefore any help with loans or grants, as in development areas, might help sway a decision on the location of a plant.

Table 13.1 The importance of different location factors in various industries

Industry	Location factor								
	Near power	Near raw materials	Near market	External economics	Government intervention	Political situation	Climate	Near to commercial centres	Transport
Car industry	A	B	B/C	A	A/B	A	C	B	B
Brick manufacture	A	A	A	B	B	B	C	B	A
Construction	C	B	A/C	B	B/C	A	B	B	B
Shipbuilding	B	B	C	A	A	B	C	B	A
Electronics									
Jewellery									
Craft industries									

A = very important; B = fairly important; C = not very important

As so much money is at stake in capital investment, car production plants are unlikely to be set up in politically volatile countries.

Climate, as in most factory-based industries, is of secondary importance, although in other countries extremes of heat and cold can cause the expenditure of much energy on air conditioning or heating.

Brick manufacture

The firing of bricks uses a great deal of energy, whatever form of fuel is used. Traditionally it was coal, and very often coal was mined on the same site as the clay. Modern methods, however, use oil fired kilns, and so nearness to energy sources is not so important today in Britain.

Bricks have a low cost/weight ratio. As the total cost is still relatively low, then much money cannot be spent on the transport of heavy raw materials, or finished goods. Traditionally bricks were manufactured on the site of the clay workings, and this still goes on a great deal today. The transport of finished bricks is almost invariably by lorry, and many brickworks have an economic distribution area of only a few tens of kilometres, before their delivery costs become higher than those of a nearer competitor.

The government can chiefly affect the brick industry, by whether or not it allows the extraction of clay in a certain area. It could be argued that extraction of clay would expand employment but mar the countryside. (An ideal situation for the use of cost—benefit analysis (CBA).)

Brick manufacture in less developed countries is a fairly stable industry necessary to the local environment. It is unlikely to be affected greatly by politically volatile situations: much less so than, say, a car assembly plant, where components may be imported, and finished cars exported.

Construction

The location of the construction industry needs to be viewed in a different light to other industries, as the industry will always be found where work is needed to be done. The reason for this is, of course, that the products of the construction industry are not mobile. Therefore given any flourishing sector of business, the construction industry will be there, building factories, houses or service buildings.

Although there are many power tools used on construction sites, any site, if necessary, could become self-contained from the power point of view.

The construction industry could in some respects be looked upon as a service industry, as it provides the service of constructing buildings or other structures where the client wants them. The choice of position is the client's, and is often made with a view to long-term operation of the building:

(a) If a factory, it may be near markets or raw materials.
(b) If an office block, it may be within a commercial centre, close to passenger transport facilities.
(c) If a private house, the position and views over the countryside may be of prime importance.

The actual cost of the construction is often of secondary importance to these examples of other factors, and as any building material can be transported anywhere, the closeness to raw materials is not critical.

The closeness to market becomes more important, the smaller the construction business. As discussed in Chapter 9, a maintenance builder has to operate within a fairly small geographical market, whereas a constructor of motorways operates nationally.

The political situation in countries abroad, where firms foreign to that country have secured contracts, is most important. Many companies have carried out such contracts, only to discover that final payments are held up indefinitely, or that actual war or government intervention has caused the closure of the site.

Climate can affect construction sites, but if a building is required in a climatically bad area, then this is just reflected in the price.

Shipbuilding

The most fundamental factor in the siting of this industry is that it should be on the coast, and adjacent to water deep enough to allow the transporting of the finished vessels.

The need for power is fairly important, particularly in the initial stages of cutting and shaping of steel etc.

The nearness to markets is not all that critical, as orders in Britain are obtained from many foreign countries.

External economies are especially important, particularly with regard to having a trained labour force nearby.

As shipbuilding is nearly always centred in development areas in this country, the government is under considerable pressure to maintain employment in this area.

In the past in this country, and today in certain countries abroad, pressure could be exerted by the government to establish shipbuilding facilities, either to produce warships for defence, or cargo ships, which would cut out the need to buy from abroad.

The above descriptions of the four industries have been fairly brief, as it was intended to give only the major factors concerned with industrial location.

The relative importance of the various factors in the particular industries will not remain static, as commerce, politics, social effects, communications and transport are changing constantly. What today may be a major factor, tomorrow may be insignificant.

Question

1 Complete Table 13.1, and discuss reasons for your weightings.

Chapter 14

Types of business enterprise and their financing

Introduction

Business enterprises can exist in one of several forms — sole traders, partnerships, companies, nationalised industries — all of which are described below.

The choice of business enterprise will depend upon three basic factors, to which are related many others.

(a) The size of the business operation is an important factor, for this will determine the amount of capital required, the need for experienced specialists in the various functions of the enterprise, and the number of managers, and possibly owners of the business.

(b) The type of product being produced is another major factor. This is partly linked with (a) above, in that the type of product often dictates the scale of operations possible in a particular field. Woodcarving, for instance, would not take the form of a large-scale operation, whereas standard joinery manufacture would.

(c) The degree of risk associated with the enterprise. The construction industry in particular is prone to a high level of bankruptcies and insolvencies. The prudent businessman would opt for a business type which enjoyed limited liability. Limited liability is a situation where the financial liability of the owner is limited to a certain figure and where all personal possessions – e.g. cars, house, furniture etc. – would not normally be in jeopardy should the business fail.

Sole traders

This is the simplest form of organisation, and it exists where there is one owner of a business.

It may take the form of a one-man business, where no other people are employed, or the owner may employ several people to work for him. This form of business is very common in small building firms, as it is an ideal type of unit for carrying out small works.

Little capital is required and this is usually provided by the owner, or through limited borrowing from banks.

Small businesses of this type are very flexible, in that the owner can quickly make decisions, and as the organisational structure is small, communications

One major problem with this form of organisation is the fact that there is unlimited personal liability for any debts incurred.

Advantages of sole traders

(a) It is easy to start this form of business.
(b) Little capital is required.
(c) The owner can work as hard as he wants to, for the rewards are all his.
(d) There are good communications, and personal contact with staff and customers.
(e) The business is flexible, due to small organisation and fast decision-making.

Disadvantages of sole traders

(a) Scope of activities has limits set by experience of the owner.
(b) Problems of administration when the owner is ill, or on holiday.
(c) Expansion is limited, as further capital is often difficult to obtain.
(d) Unlimited liability exists for debts incurred.

Partnerships

A partnership may be formed by two or more people, generally up to a maximum of 20. Partnerships are often formed by sole traders taking on a partner to form a partnership, between the original sole trader and the newcomer. The new partner would be chosen for his ability to provide additional skills or money. A partnership can be formed with just a verbal agreement, but it is advisable to have drawn up a proper partnership agreement, to include such items as:

(a) the duration of the partnership
(b) the amount of capital each partner will contribute
(c) the allocation of profits and losses
(d) amounts of salaries of each partner
(e) how any dispute between the partners will be settled
(f) the nature of the firms' business
(g) the names of the partners
(h) the commencement date of the partnership and terms of notice for termination

Ordinary partnerships help to spread the load of responsibility, but because all partners are responsible for the actions of an individual partner, it is essential to ensure that they are trustworthy, and act in a reasonable manner. With partnerships, there is still unlimited liability, so that if one particular partner incurs debts on the partnership's behalf, then the personal possessions of all the other partners could be claimed in payment.

It is possible to form a limited partnership. In this case, at least one partner must still be accountable for the partnership debts, whilst the other limited partners enjoy limited liability. This means that they will not be asked to pay more money than they have agreed to invest, should debts be incurred.

A business run as a partnership lacks permanence, for if one partner dies, the whole partnership has to be dissolved, and recreated in a different form.

Many professional firms, such as architects, quantity surveyors etc. are run as partnerships.

Advantages of partnerships

(a) A partnership is fairly easy to form.
(b) It allows for the combination of the different skills of the partners.
(c) It provides a method of obtaining a financial backer.
(d) It eases the administrative load, compared with that of a sole trader.

Disadvantages of partnerships

(a) There is unlimited liability.
(b) A great degree of personal harmony is required between the partners.

Companies

A company can exist as one of three types, and in either a public or private form.

Private companies have between two and 50 shareholders. They do not have to publish a balance sheet, although they do have to send in copies of accounts to The Registrar of Companies, Companies House, Crown Way, Cardiff, and for a nominal sum these can be inspected by the public. The sale and transfer of shares in private companies may be restricted so that the general public does not gain access to a small, tightly controlled business.

Public companies have at least two shareholders, with no maximum number being stipulated. Balance sheets are published in the press, and there is no restriction on the sale or transfer of shares. The company name must end in PLC (public limited company). The memorandum must state that the company is to be a public company and it must have an authorised capital of not less than £50 000.

Private companies can be formed as:

1. *Unlimited companies.* These are quite unusual organisations and may exist when a company has no liabilities but only holds assets. Its main advantage is that the company does not have to send a copy of its accounts to the company registrar.
2. *Companies limited by guarantee.* Here the members guarantee to provide a certain sum of money should the company go into liquidation. This type of company is generally not involved in normal business activities but generally it is operating as a service organisation e.g. BTEC (the Business and Technology Education Council), or a chamber of commerce.
3. *Companies limited by shares.* Here the shareholder's liability is limited to the total price he has agreed to pay for the shares. This category of company is by far the most important in business today.

The operation of these limited companies can be very simply described as follows.

People purchase shares in the company, and should the company make a profit, the directors decide what proportion of the profit will be allocated to the shareholders as dividend. The dividend is expressed as a percentage of the fully paid-up face value of the share. Whilst the shareholders are the owners of the company, the actual policies of the company are laid down by the board of directors,which is selected by the shareholders. Should the directors fail to declare a dividend one year, although a profit was made, then possibly the directors' jobs will be in jeopardy.

The normal day-to-day running of the company is controlled by the managing director, who is a member of the board. Under him is the normal business organisational structure, which varies according to the size of the enterprise.

A limited company is seen in law as a separate legal entity, and is able to 'sign' contracts and be sued in its own right. A company also enjoys permanence, for a company is not affected by the death of a shareholder, as the shares simply pass to the heir. The company itself stays in business until it is liquidated, either compulsorily, or voluntarily. A company can plan ahead for longer periods in the knowledge that its existence is not dependent upon the skills of one, or a few people.

The formation of a company offers the ability to acquire much more capital than a partnership or sole trader, and public companies can obtain much more than private companies, as they are open to wider subscription. Investors will be willing to invest, knowing that their risk is limited to the amount they agree to pay. It provides a means whereby a large amount of capital can be accumulated, for large capital-intensive projects, from many relatively small investors.

Public companies can only be formed as companies limited by shares.

Advantages of limited companies

(a) Limited liability means that the personal possessions of the owners are not at risk.
(b) It provides a means whereby people can invest small or large amounts, without the worry of being involved in the running of the business.
(c) It enables businesses to grow quickly. In the past, businesses often grew as a result of the ploughing back of profits. Today with greater competition resulting in lower profits, it is often essential to start off at a large scale of operation. This needs much capital.
(d) A limited company has perpetual life.
(e) People often have more faith when dealing with a limited company.
(f) Mergers and takeovers are relatively easy with public limited companies, as valuations are more easily arrived at through reference to the quoted share values.
(g) The company is not dependent upon the knowledge or skill of any individual. Any specialist can in theory be hired by the company, in any capacity.
(h) The shares of public companies are dealt with on the stock exchange. This means that the shares in such companies can be easily converted into cash, although the value of the shares on the day of sale has to be accepted.
(i) In public companies, there are often facilities for investment, with varying degrees of risk and profit potential (see the section on types of shares).

Disadvantages of limited companies

(a) It involves following a strict procedure for formation and operation, as laid down in the 1985 and 1989 Companies Acts.
(b) Some degree of privacy is lost, as any member of the public can obtain financial details from The Registrar of Companies.
(c) There is often disagreement between the shareholders and the directors, on matters of policy. Thus the divorce of control from ownership is not always a good thing. The directors have to look after the interests of the company. The shareholders primarily look after the interests of their investment, and are often more concerned about their dividends than future expansion of the company.

Formation of a limited company

The Companies Acts require that those wishing to form a limited company should supply the following documents to the Registrar of Companies together with the necessary registration fee and the stamp duty payable on the nominal capital.

1. *The Memorandum of Association.* This contains information defining the company's relation with the factors outside the business.
    The following points should be included:

    - *The company name.* The Registrar may refuse to register any undesirable name, or one which is misleading.
    - *The address of the registered office.* All legal and statutory information will then be sent to that office. The European Communities Act 1972 now requires that the registered office address is shown on all business letters and order forms.
    - *The objects clause.* This sets out the type of activities of the company. It is necessary to include everything that the company might wish to become involved with in the future, as well as the present, for a company cannot legally operate outside its range of operations as defined in the objects.
    - *The limited liability clause.* This will state whether the company is limited by shares or guarantee. If by shares, then there will be a statement to the effect that the total liability is limited to the fully paid-up value of the shares. If by guarantee, then the terms of the guarantee will be laid down.
    - *The capital clause.* This sets out the nominal or authorised share capital of the company, and its division into the different types of shares. As stamp duty is payable generally at the rate of 1 per cent of nominal capital, then there is some incentive to keep the nominal capital to a realistic figure.
    - *Signature.* The Memorandum must be signed by at least two people for a private company, or seven people if for a public company.

2. *The Articles of Association.* These relate to the internal workings of the company's activities. The rights and duties of members (shareholders) are set out, concerning the sale and transfer of shares. The procedure for voting and the rules for holding various meetings are laid down, as are the method of appointment and removal of directors and the determination of their salaries.
    Information relating to dividends and reserves should also be included.

3. *A statement of names and particulars.* This consists of the names and full particulars of the first directors and first secretary together with their signatures, stating that they are willing to act in the capacity indicated.

4. *A Statutory Declaration.* This is a declaration usually signed by the solicitor forming the company, stating that the various Companies Acts have been complied with.

5. *A statement of capital.* This merely states the value of authorised or nominal capital of the company.

Providing all the documents are in order, then the Registrar will issue a certificate of incorporation, after which the company must acquire the capital with which to start trading. A private company will generally have subscribers already waiting, often the directors, and the money will be available almost immediately.

Public companies have to follow a different path, however. A prospectus is issued by advertising in the national press, requesting the public to subscribe. Included in the prospectus are the names of the company directors and the number, value and nature of the shares. The minimum subscription must also be stated in the case of the first share issue of a company. This is the minimum amount of money that the company can operate with initially. If this minimum subscription is not obtained by a certain date, then all monies received for shares have to be returned, and the particular share issue is void.

Public companies might not require all their nominal capital at once, in which case only part of it will be obtained initially, and a second and possibly a third issue of shares will be made at a later date. With these later share issues, the prospectuses must include:

(a) a report of the profits and losses over the preceding five years, and the assets and liabilities at the last balancing date
(b) the dividends declared over the last five years
(c) if another business is to be purchased with the proceeds of the share issue, then the information about that particular business as in (a) and (b) above is required

Company capital

As was explained at the beginning of the book, there are different definitions of capital. In this section capital will be taken to mean the financial resources of the company. Even with this definition however, there may still be some confusion, for the capital of a company could refer either to the working capital or to various types of capital related to the share structure of the company, as follows:

- *Nominal, authorised or registered capital.* This is the full amount of capital which the company may issue shares for, as in the Memorandum.
- *Issued or subscribed capital.* The total value of the shares allotted, whether actually paid up or not. It is not necessary to issue shares for the total of the nominal capital, so the issued capital is that part of the nominal capital for which shares have been issued.
- *Called-up capital.* The amount of the issued capital which the directors have asked to be paid at this time. When shares are bought, the full price is not always asked for immediately. This often makes it easier to sell the shares. The called-up capital is this amount that should have been paid.
- *Uncalled capital.* That part of the issued capital that does not have to be paid at this time.
- *Paid-up capital.* The amount of called-up capital that has actually been paid. The difference between called-up capital and paid-up capital is known as calls in arrears.

- *Unissued capital.* That part of nominal capital not yet issued.
- *Reserve capital.* Capital set aside out of uncalled capital, which will only be called in for use if the company is wound up.

The above definitions can be better explained by the following example.

Example: A newly formed company has a nominal capital of £100 000, and decides to issue 60 000 £1 shares, of which 75p per share is payable immediately, and 10p per share is set aside as a reserve. At the present time, only £37 000 of the £45 000 called up, has actually been paid.

Nominal authorised or registered capital	100 000
Issued capital	60 000
Unissued capital is therefore	40 000
Issued capital	60 000
Called-up capital	45 000
Uncalled capital is therefore	15 000

Of this £15 000, £6000 is reserve capital, which leaves £9000 to be called in at some future date.

Called-up capital	45 000
Paid-up capital	37 000
Calls in arrears is therefore	8 000

Shares

A company may have issued only one type of share, or several different types. All shares, however, fall into two main types.

1. Ordinary shares. These are the most common type of share issued. They are the risk type shares, for dividends may be high or low or, at certain times, non-existent. It is the holders of such shares that are the financial risk-takers of industry today.

Ordinary shares do not qualify for a fixed percentage dividend, for the return per share may fluctuate wildly between good and bad years. The dividend on ordinary shares is payable after that for any preference shares.

Ordinary shares are sometimes subdivided into deferred ordinary and preferred ordinary. Preferred ordinary are paid their dividend before the deferred ordinary.

2. Preference shares. These have preference over ordinary shares, with regard to dividends. Preference shares are designated by a fixed rate of dividend payable, which has to be paid in full before ordinary shares are allocated a dividend. In the absence of any provision to the contrary in the articles, all preference shares are cumulative. This means that if there is insufficient money to pay the guaranteed dividend on the preference shares in a particular year, then next year the shareholders will receive any back dividend due, plus the current dividend.

Under normal circumstances, if a company has made good profits one year, the preference shareholders get their expected dividend, with probably a high dividend for any ordinary shareholders.

Participating preference shares again receive their guaranteed dividend, but once the ordinary shareholders have received a certain amount, the rest of the allocated profits are distributed between the participating preference shareholders and the ordinary shareholders in a predetermined manner.

The payment to the shareholder, for the risk of investing his money, is the dividend he receives. This is expressed as a percentage of the fully paid-up face value of the share. The total amount of profits allocated to dividends is decided by the board of directors. It is important to note that dividends must come out of profits.

To try to determine the profitability of a company by looking at its share capital structure, or the dividend paid, is not really possible. The nominal or issued capital gives little indication of the size of the company's operations, for it may be financing itself from past profits, or from other sources of borrowed capital. A statement of the percentage dividend offered has to be investigated carefully. A 20 per cent dividend may sound very good, but this may have been for a share whose face value was £1, whereas if the company has been doing well and has shown good dividends in the past, the shareholder may have had to pay £2 for this share on the stock market. The actual dividend is 20 per cent of £1 or 20p. This represents a return on the shareholders investment of only 10 per cent.

Conversely, if the shareholder only paid 50p for the share, his actual return is 40 per cent.

The Stock Exchange

The Stock Exchange is a market for second-hand shares. Fully listed companies are now graded as alpha, beta or gamma stocks, where alpha are the most actively traded and gamma the least.

If a member of the public wished to buy shares in, say, ICI, then he/she could approach a broker, which might be a firm of stockbrokers or a high street bank. The broker then consults an SEAQ (Stock Exchange automated quotations system) monitor which will indicate which market makers (the firms that actually make a market in the shares) operate in these stocks. In some instances the broker and the market maker will be different divisions of the same firm; however, in-house transactions are strictly controlled to avoid buying or selling which would be disadvantageous to the client. The broker then makes a deal with the market maker and the transaction is recorded.

The broker obtains his income from the commission on sales whilst the market maker obtains a profit from the difference between his selling price and buying price.

The prices of shares fluctuate, depending upon the supply and demand of individual shares. If a company is making good profits, or indeed if there is only a rumour of good profits, then people will want to buy shares in that company. People already owning the shares, however, will not want to sell, hence the market price for the shares will be high. If a company does not seem to be producing good dividends, then the share values will be low. The prices of the shares are listed daily in the national newspapers, but the most detailed information is to be found in the *Financial Times*.

The importance of the stock market to industry is that it ensures that investors will be willing to invest money in company shares, with the knowledge that their investment can be easily converted back into cash if they so wish. Besides shares, the Stock Exchange deals in stocks, which are another form of investment, but which are normally offered in this form initially by government, nationalised industries, local authorities etc. to finance capital projects.

Working capital

This is capital needed to finance the day-to-day running of the company, to buy materials and pay salaries and wages, until customers pay their debts.

The majority of the share capital of a company is used to purchase the long-term assets of the company, such as the premises and plant. There will occasionally be times when, due to recession, or after an expansion programme that has been financed from past profits, the company will be short of funds, and will need to seek sources of finance.

Sources of finance

When considering finance for a business the type of finance required will be categorised as:

(a) Short term. That required for up to 3 years.
(b) Medium term. That required for 3–10 years.
(c) Long term. That required for over 10 years.

It should be noted that the following sections are aimed fairly specifically at the construction industry, and many points may not be applicable to other industries.

When a company decides that it is short of funds, the managers' first thought is often to go out and seek a loan of some kind. There are however certain checks that should be made on company finances before this step is taken. A few examples follow.

Example 1: Many small to medium construction companies own their own plant. This results in the tying up of large sums of money in capital items for which work may not always be available. There will also be money invested in the maintaining of a plant yard, together with service and stores facilities. Many such companies, after detailed analysis, have found it more economical to cut down on the amount of plant they own, which leads to considerable savings. The action of selling off plant, and possibly the yard, can also give a useful boost to working capital, and forestall the need for further finance.

Example 2: All builders maintain a yard or stores compound, either at head office or on site. If the level of stocks rises too high for the particular work being undertaken, then they should be reduced. Perhaps high stock levels are due to an over-enthusiastic ordering surveyor, who has tried to obtain very low prices, but has resulted in overbuying. Whatever the reason, if stocks can be reduced, then working capital will no longer be tied up.

Example 3:   Medium to large companies often run specialist sections which might include such areas of activity as site investigation, plumbing, electrical work etc. A constant check should be kept on the profitability of the individual specialist areas, for it is sometimes the case that several profitable areas are having to carry one or two sections that constantly make losses. If this is so, then after due consideration the unprofitable sections should be disbanded. This may seem an obvious action, but it is surprising how often companies allow this situation to develop and continue.

Example 4:   An analysis of cash flow within the company might reveal that those clients owing money to the company are taking longer to pay their bills than is reasonable.

This problem might be solved by becoming firmer with the bad payers, or even operating on pro forma invoices. By this method the client pays before the work is carried out. Another method gaining popularity is that of factoring the company's invoices. Here the factoring company buys all the company's invoices at a discount, and takes over the responsibility of administering invoices and statements etc. and collects the money from the clients. The advantage of this is that the company gets its money very quickly, and it can also often cut down on the administrative staff.

The period of credit given by the company's suppliers is also of the utmost importance. The majority of goods supplied are on monthly account, which means that to qualify for discount, usually $2\frac{1}{2}$ per cent, the goods have to be paid for by the end of the month following delivery. By ensuring that goods are ordered in the first week of the next month rather than the last week of the present month, and also by ensuring no goods are purchased for cash, economies can be made.

Example 5:   The hiring, rather than the owning, of plant has already been mentioned. In many companies the philosophy of contract hire has been extended to include office equipment, cars, offices, even staff; this inevitably leads to less capital being tied up.

Short-term finance

Not until sources of internal economies and financial resources have been fully investigated should external sources be sought.

Short-term finance may be needed to cover periods when a contractor wants to take on or set up another contract. It can also cover short-term cash-flow problems, where a client's payment is overdue. This form of finance can also be used to purchase land for development, or plant for a particular job.

Traditionally, the bank overdraft has been the most popular form of short-term finance. With this method, the bank manager gives agreement to a maximum overdraft figure for the company's account. Very often some form of security is needed for this facility. With an overdraft, the company only pays interest on the actual amount of the overdraft used, not the total overdraft figure granted. For example, if a company had an overdraft facility for £100 000, but at a particular time its overdraft was only £40 000, then at that time, interest would only be payable on the £40 000. The interest payable is generally about 2 per cent above bank base rates (BR), and overdraft facilities are generally reviewed annually.

Bank loans are another source of finance often used. Here the bank credits the account of the company with the amount in question, and the company has to begin repaying the loan with interest on the total figure borrowed, straight away, whether or not the money is being used by the company.

Overdraft interest fluctuates, following the movements of the BR, whilst interest payable on a loan is usually fixed for the period of the loan. Hence it is often better to take out a loan when BR is low, but likely to rise, whilst it is better to take out an overdraft when BR is high, and likely to drop.

Hire purchase is a form of short-term finance often used to buy capital items such as plant etc. With this method, the machine can be purchased, and set to work to start earning profit for the company, before it is finally paid for. By careful planning, this often works out very well.

Deferred creditors are those with long periods between payments. A typical example is the Inland Revenue. Here payment of VAT and PAYE etc. is only made every few months. The money set aside for these payments can be used to finance short-term ventures, providing the money will be available when required.

Medium-term finance

This is said to be one of the most difficult forms of finance to obtain. High-street banks are reluctant to invest money for periods of up to ten years, and very often if the money is needed for only three to eight years it is not really worth offering a new share issue to the public.

Finance can often be arranged from commercial banks, or finance houses, but at a fairly high rate of interest, and often they insist on a seat on the board of directors, just to ensure that the company will be managed properly.

Funds over the medium to long term can be provided by various finance corporations. Investors in Industry (known as the 3i) invests in a wide range of industries. Investors in Industry is owned by the clearing banks and the Bank of England. There are other finance corporations such as the Agricultural Mortgage Corporation, Equity Capital for Industry and the Commonwealth Development Corporation.

The National Enterprise Board, which used to assist industry with funds, was amalgamated with the National Research Development Group in 1981 to form the British Technology Group (BTG). The main function of the Group is to promote the development of technology arising from such public sector sources as universities, polytechnics, research councils and various government establishments. BTG follows an invention right through from development and funding to industrial production.

Long-term finance

There are several main sources of long-term finance.

1. Increasing the issued capital of the company: This involves the floating of a new share issue on the market. In order for this venture to be a success, the company must have a good past record of dividends in order to tempt investors to buy shares. With a public company, a prospectus will be placed in national newspapers. With private companies, further shares can only be issued in accordance with the articles, which normally insist on the full agreement of the existing shareholders.

It must be remembered that the nominal capital, as stated in the memorandum, is the maximum that can be issued. If more than this is required, then the nominal capital figure will have to be changed by a special meeting of shareholders.

If there is any uncalled capital outstanding on existing share issues, then it may be possible to call this in.

2. Debentures: The traditional form of long-term finance is the debenture. A debenture is a loan, generally a secured loan, and must not be confused with shares, which are concerned with the ownership of the company. Most shares carry voting rights, but debentures do not. A debenture is a fixed-interest security, and in modern industry, they are generally repayable before a certain date, or very occasionally they may be irredeemable during the existence of the company.

A debenture loan may be raised by an issue open to public subscription, or a debenture may be granted by a bank, insurance or pension fund, or finance house. The debenture holder does not share in the risks of the company, for the interest must be paid, whether a profit is made or not. As the risk is less than that of owning shares, the return is generally less.

In order that a company may secure a debenture loan it must, over the long period, expect to make at least enough profit to pay off the interest. Also the company should possess assets which are unlikely to depreciate greatly.

The most usual form of debenture found in business today is the mortgage debenture. Under this form, the debenture is secured by the mortgage of a specific asset (usually land, premises, or sometimes large plant).

Floating debentures are also occasionally used. With this type of loan, it is secured by a charge on all, or certain sections of, the company's assets.

In theory, unsecured debentures can exist, and these are known as simple or naked debentures, and are mere promises to pay, with no security given. In practice, as one would imagine, they are not seen very often.

Companies may make one debenture issue, or many. In the latter case, they are often designated A, B, or C debentures to indicate their order of priority. Generally the lower the priority the greater the rate of interest, to compensate for the lower degree of security.

3. The retention of past profits: Instead of distributing past profits in the form of dividends etc. they may be retained in order to build up a capital reserve within the company.

Depreciation allowances: Government allows business to depreciate or write off a certain proportion of assets. For example a proportion of plant purchased in a particular year can be put against profits, before taxation is calculated. The accumulated additions of these tax savings over the years create a useful pool of finance for the business.

Local authorities: In many areas local authorities encourage new investment in development projects, and for some types of activity long-term loans are available.

Finance for building projects

Many of the previous forms of finance discussed above can be used to finance property development. The type of finance obviously depends upon whether the building will be sold immediately it is finished, in which case the loan will be repaid quickly. Alternatively, the building may be owned by the developing company, and rented or leased to an occupier. With this latter situation longer-term finance is required than with the former.

With housing development, at certain times, building societies will help finance the cost of erection of the dwellings, by giving stage payments to the builder as the work progresses. When the property is sold, the builder pays off the loan to the building society, and the buyer's building society takes over paying the stage payments, if the house is still not completed.

Where a company decides to move into larger office or factory accommodation, finance can sometimes be arranged with pension or insurance funds. With this method, the pension fund will pay for the construction by monthly payments, or at negotiated stages. On the completion of the structure, a lease will be signed with the occupying company. The pension fund remains the owner of a valuable appreciating asset, whilst the occupiers have effectively leased a new building tailor-made to suit their requirements.

The cost of finance

The choice of source of finance for a business depends largely on the activities undertaken. A large engineering factory needs to have a great deal of capital tied up in fixed assets for long periods. This necessitates much long-term finance. Similarly for a property developer erecting buildings for rent, as the ownership of the properties remained with the company, again much long-term finance would be needed.

A building company involved in general contracting has very few fixed long-term assets by comparison with the previous examples. There may be a head office building and an amount of plant. The vast majority of its work, however, could be financed by short-term means.

Once the capital structure of the business has been decided upon, i.e. whether it is mainly long or short term, then the source of funds should be considered.

With short-term funding the interest rate considerations over the period of the loan must be projected. As previously stated, bank loans are at fixed rates of interest, whereas bank overdrafts fluctuate with interest rates. If interest rates are expected to fall from present levels and stay low, then overdrafts might be cheaper than loans, and vice versa.

With long-term funding one has to consider how long the funding is probably required and the effect this will have on profitability.

Debentures are generally for fixed periods of 5–25 years and interest is paid before taxation is considered. Compare this to a new share issue. This is much more expensive than a debenture to carry out. It means more shares within the company will need a dividend throughout the life of the company, with the dividend being found out of profits *after* tax.

In reality a company will have to compare the costs of the various types of finance, a general rule of thumb being to have shares issued to the value of capital that is certain always to be required, and for periods when excessive capital is needed debentures can be used.

Questions

1 What type of business enterprise is best for the construction industry?
2 Suggest what problems might be encountered if it was proposed that the construction industry should be nationalised.
3 Discuss the main differences between bank loans, ordinary shares, and debentures.
4 Suggest why it would be inadvisable to use a new share issue for a short-term loan.

Chapter 15

Government objectives and their attainment

Introduction

A government is generally chosen because its policies represent those required by the majority of the voting population of the country. It is not surprising therefore to find that the main objectives of government are those concerned with improving the general conditions for the population.

This chapter will discuss the various objectives, and show their inter-relationships with one another. Chapters 16–18 will show in detail the methods used to try to achieve these ends, and Chapter 19 will discuss in particular how application of these methods affects the construction industry.

In this chapter five government objectives will be considered: improvement of living standards; high level of employment; redistribution of wealth; curbing of inflation; good balance of payments.

Improvement of living standards

This is a very vague title, and can mean many things. There are, however, two factors that will be considered.

Improvement in the real earnings of society

An improvement in real earnings is said to have taken place if a salary will buy more goods this year than last. An actual comparison of salary or wage figures over a succession of years gives very little information unless the level of inflation (the rise in the price of goods), has been taken into account.

An improvement in real earnings can only come about by economic growth. This should ultimately result in greater productivity, and more efficient working practices.

Social welfare and the environment

Although increased real earnings can improve the material surroundings of one's home, it can have little direct effect on social costs and benefits of society generally.

Pollution is one problem that affects people's lives. It should be remembered that pollution is not just oily beaches but it also includes:

* noisy environment
* dusty or smoky atmosphere
* dirty streets
* polluted waterways
* contaminated land

Even the encroachment of the urban sprawl on natural areas is a form of pollution.

Although pollution is often caused by individuals, only government can pass legislation to curtail it. It is ironic that economic growth often results in greater pollution, and because the prevention of industrial pollution can be expensive, it is often not put into practice until government demands it.

There are many social benefits which could be included in the improving of living standards. These might include:

* the peace of mind given, by knowing there is a good police force or army in existence
* the operation of an efficient health service
* state benefit and pension schemes
* libraries and education services

Government still has fairly direct control over these areas, by passing the relevant legislation, or by increasing budgets for these schemes. Government, however, has little direct control over the improvement of earnings, only the more efficient operation of industry and commerce can help here.

High level of employment

This is related to the real earning capacity of society. If unemployment drops, then society as a whole earns more money with which to purchase goods. In turn, the purchase of goods can lead to higher output from industry, which leads to more jobs.

High unemployment can lead to certain problems.

(a) As fewer people are employed, the government loses income in the form of income tax, and national insurance contributions which can not now be collected from those out of work. At the same time, unemployment benefits are paid out to these people, which throws a much greater burden on the reduced working force. It can be seen that should unemployment become too great, then the whole system of taxation and benefits and services could break down. The problem is similar to that of an ageing population. In such a situation, as the age structure of the population gets older, there are fewer workers to support the growing number of elderly.

(b) Many people feel a sense of personal loss of dignity when unemployed. Traditionally people choose a career and could spend all their working lives within their chosen industry. Today because of developing technology, changing business methods and manufacturing bases within economies, people should expect to have to change their career direction at least once within their working lives.

(c) There can be undesirable side effects, such as an increase in vandalism and petty crimes. This in itself leads to more money being spent on preventing and remedying these problems.

Redistribution of wealth

In any society, there will be certain sectors whose relative earnings lag behind those of others. This is particularly relevant to people who do not or cannot take industrial action to force high wage settlements.

At the same time, there are certain other sectors of society who receive particularly high salaries. Government tries to even out the inequalities to a certain extent by taxing the higher paid, whilst the lower paid pay less tax and possibly even receive government benefits, to boost incomes.

Many people are of the belief that heavily taxing the higher paid takes away the incentive to work, as a greater percentage of the income is taken away as tax. Another criticism often voiced is that paying benefits to the lower paid and unemployed encourages people to work less, if at all.

The controlling of inflation

Over a period of time the monetary cost of goods or services rises. This increase is known as inflation. The retail price index is measured by comparing, over a twelve-month period, the costs of a 'basket' of commodities purchased by the mass of the population. The actual calculation and weighting of the many different commodities is quite complex and actually changes from time to time. This makes direct comparison between figures now and in the past a little difficult. Everyone is aware of the effects of inflation; it increases all materials costs, from bricks and cement, to the cost of land. Inevitably it leads to high wage demands in order to keep pace. What causes these increases in costs?

Economists talk of two situations leading to inflationary tendencies:

Demand inflation

This is where too much money is chasing too few goods, and by the action of supply and demand, the price of the relatively scarce goods rises. This can most easily be seen to take place, to a limited extent, when there is a high demand for certain commodities, e.g.:

(a) candles in a power cut
(b) sugar when there is a sugar shortage
(c) collectors' items in general

Within Britain at the present time it is unlikely that there is a considerable shortage of goods, so it is doubtful whether this is the main cause for inflation in this country. In some countries, however, this can be seen to be the main cause. In some cities in Russia in the early 1990s there were severe food shortages which forced up the prices of many goods, some of which were only available on the black market.

Cost inflation

This is brought about by a rise in the price of goods leading to a demand for higher wages to compensate for this increased cost of goods. The increased wages then lead to further increases in commodity prices and so on. This continues as an ever-increasing spiral. One problem with this theory is that inflation tends to go up at a faster rate than it should, by just taking wages into account. It must be remembered that part of the cost of a commodity is made up of the raw material input. Another factor is that, at times, the increasing cost of interest rates and dividends needed to be paid to finance industry can increase inflation (Fig. 15.1).

Ironically government often helps to fuel inflation, rather than cure it, by imposing high interest rates, and especially by imposing high taxes, particularly on fuels. An increase in the tax on petrol or diesel fuel immediately increases

Fig. 15.1 Factors of inflation

the cost of all goods which have to be transported; this increase is inevitably passed on to the consumer eventually.

Maintaining a good balance of payments

The balance of payments is a measure of the ability of Britain's exports to balance its imports. A surplus balance of payments means that Britain has exported more than it has imported.

If, on the other hand, Britain's imports exceeded the exports, then if this continued for a long period, economic decline would probably occur.

The balance of payments is discussed more thoroughly in Chapter 18.

Methods of attaining government objectives

It is difficult to see how improvement could be made to social benefits. At present, with many it is necessary only to maintain the *status quo*. Admittedly it might be possible to improve the health service, or the education facilities, but it is doubtful whether an increase in the number of libraries, for instance, could really be justified. An increase in certain areas might even have a detrimental effect. If, for instance, the police or army were greatly increased, an extreme condition might arise, as has occurred in certain countries, in that a police state might emerge, with the loss of individual freedom.

The whole sphere of social benefits is under the direct control of government, via legislation and budgets. The types of benefits provided will, however, only be a reflection of those required by the population, for government, after all, is guided by the majority in a democracy.

Growth in real income can only come about by economic growth, and this is usually possible only during a period of low inflation. There are various degrees and mixes of policies, adopted by governments, in trying to control inflation, whilst at the same time trying to stimulate growth. They can, however, be simplified into three basic policies, which are adopted in varying degrees of intensity.

Keynesian policy

In the 1930s, Lord Keynes developed and published his famous general theory. This used the idea of stimulating an economy in which there was high unemployment back into a growth situation. His idea was that central government could stimulate the economy in two ways:

(a) By placing more government contracts, and generally expanding the amount of work executed in the public sector. This would lead directly to more workers being required to carry out the jobs, and so more money would be earned, which in turn meant more goods would be bought, and so the growth would continue.

(b) The alternative would be to lower taxation rates, thus effectively putting more money into the pockets of the consumers. They would spend the increase in money, causing a general increase in consumer demand which results in the need to produce more. In this way, more jobs would be created, which again would lead to continuing growth.

Both of the above policies would result in the government operating a budget deficit. This means that the government's income was less than its expenditure. Chapter 16 discusses this further.

The injection of investment into an economy leads to the multiplier effect. For example, an injection of money as supplied by the Keynesian policy leads to more employment and higher earnings. If these increased earnings are spent quickly, then more goods have to be produced more quickly. If the money continues to be spent and not saved, then it can be seen that the circular flow of money has caused the initial investment to 'multiply' several times. This ability to spend quickly rather than save is known as the marginal propensity to consume (MPC).

If, for instance, a person spent three quarters of a wage increase then the MPC would be $\frac{3}{4}$. Alternatively it can be said that the marginal propensity to save (MPS) is $1 - \frac{3}{4} = \frac{1}{4}$.

The multiplier in this example is

$$\frac{1}{\text{marginal propensity to save}} = \frac{1}{\frac{1}{4}} = 4.$$

An increase of £1 million into the economy would eventually lead to an extra £4 million in consumption.

The lower the MPS, the greater the multiplier effect. If the MPS is 0.01, then the multiplier is

$$\frac{1}{0.01} = 100$$

so that a £1 million investment would lead to £100 million of consumption.

Monetarist policy

Monetarist policy is concerned with the regulation, either directly, or indirectly, of the availability of money.

In times of high inflation, if it is more difficult for people to borrow money, or more expensive to obtain loans or credit, then they will consume less. This is achieved in various ways, but the most popular is by the Bank of England increasing the lending rate. This has the effect that banks follow the lead, and alter their base rates. As soon as this happens, building societies and other financial institutions do likewise. Besides making the borrowing of money more expensive, high interest rates make it more desirable to leave money in deposit accounts, as more interest accrues. During periods of high interest rates, in the process of trying to reduce inflation, employment nearly always suffers. For as people spend less, so less has to be produced, and so some jobs are lost.

When the government wants to stimulate growth and employment, once inflation has been brought under control, then interest rates are lowered to encourage people to consume rather than save. Once again this leads to an increased consumer demand and eventually to lower unemployment.

If it is known that demand inflation exists, by cutting back the money supply, there will be less demand, so that in theory the price of goods may drop.

Price and wage restraint policies

These forms of policy have been adopted several times, for relatively short periods, by government in the recent past. In order to bring inflation under control, restraints are brought to bear, both on manufacturers, in the amount of the price increases they can impose, and on the allowable increase of wages and salaries. The problem with this policy is that it seems to operate fairly well in the short term of say two to three years, after which time it fails, often by massive union revolt, only to see wages rising again at a rapid rate.

Whilst wage restraint is in operation, it can cause considerable hardship to the lower income groups, particularly where the allowable increases are well below the rate of inflation. A decrease in living standards can come about in such periods.

Restraint on manufacturers' price increases can seriously affect profitability, which can lead to a decrease in investment and so to slower industrial growth than would otherwise have been possible. Industry would be less inclined to invest, for two reasons:

(a) Due to low profitability, it may have to endure losses for a short period, which uses up capital that would have been used for expansion.
(b) More importantly, businessmen will see little incentive to invest, when there will be little or no return for their investment.

In these three methods of guiding the economy, there is considerable conflict between the various government objectives. It is very difficult to devise a policy which encourages an increased standard of living, with high employment and low inflation. There is no simple answer to achieving these objectives, and so the best solution is to try and maintain a reasonable balance of policies, not too extreme in their effects.

A common problem with all government policies is that a period of several months, even years in some cases, has to elapse before the outcome of a particular action can be verified. It is essential, therefore, that a government should not jump from one policy to another, before the full effect of the first has had time to operate.

Questions

1 (a) Explain with the aid of calculations how there could be a multiplier effect of 1000.
  (b) If this figure were possible, what might be the effects, following an investment by central government?
2 Find out what the main objectives of the two principal political parties are in Britain; how do they relate to those discussed in this chapter?
3 Over the last few months, what policies has the government been following; do these relate to those discussed above, and in your opinion, are they working?
4 Distinguish between demand and cost inflation, give examples when and where each of these has occurred in recent years.

Chapter 16

Fiscal control in Britain

Introduction

In Britain, and indeed in all countries, government needs to acquire funds in order to pay for a wide variety of services and projects which are supplied from central government funds.

In 1991 the total income and expenditure of the government's current account was as shown in Table 16.1.

It should be noted that the nation's fiscal year runs from 6 April to 5 April the following year.

The majority of funds to meet government expenditure come from taxation, otherwise known as fiscal measures. The levels and types of taxation are usually fixed annually on budget day, which is now in November, by the Chancellor of the Exchequer. It is the Chancellor's task, advised by many experts in the Treasury, to try to decide what levels of expenditure will exist in the various sectors of government spending over the next year. Once an estimated expenditure has been determined, then it has to be decided how the money will be raised. When deciding levels of expenditure, it is of course necessary to continue carrying out the policies of the current government, and much consultation goes on between the various departments to ensure a balanced expenditure programme. Such policies that may particularly affect decisions are: an increase of state pensions will directly affect expenditure; a pledged reduction of income tax, on the other hand will affect the means of gaining revenue.

It must be decided whether the budget will balance, or whether there will

Table 16.1 Source national income (1991) £ millions

Income		Expenditure	
Income Taxes	75 105	Defence	24 401
Taxes on expenditure	82 905	Public order etc.	3 958
Social sec. contrs	36 643	Education	1 603
Others	11 931	Health	29 076
		Social sec. benefits	57 578
		Subsidies	5 298
		Other payments	86 911
		Total expenditure	208 825
		Less deficit	2 241
	206 584		206 584

be a budget deficit. A balance indicates that income will equal the outgoings, whilst a budget deficit is where the outgoings exceed the income. In this situation the money necessary to create a balance is known as the public sector borrowing requirement (PSBR) and this may come from loans from abroad, or more usually by the issue of government stock, which is offered to the public, at a guaranteed rate of interest for fixed periods. This is in effect a loan to government by the public. It is also possible to have a budget surplus, where income exceeds expenditure.

The types of taxation can be classified under two main headings, direct and indirect.

Direct taxation

This can be defined as taxes which are paid to government, when income or wealth is received. Examples of direct taxation are given below.

Income tax

The method of taxing income in Britain is known as a progressive income tax, which means that the more a person earns, the greater will be the proportion of it that will be paid as tax. Each year most people in employment are required to fill in a tax assessment form. From the details given a certain allowance will be given for such things as being married and having certain classes of dependants. Some of the allowances might be at a lower rate than standard taxation levels. This means that a certain amount of the income will not be taxable. In order that the employer knows how much tax to deduct from the employee, the tax office allocates a tax code to the employee, based on the value of non-taxable allowances. The higher the code number, the less tax is paid.

When a person runs a business, and is not likely to know his income until the end of the year, then tax is required to be paid retrospectively for that year directly to the Inland Revenue. With the Pay As You Earn (PAYE) system the tax is deducted from an employee's wages or salary by the employer, who then passes the money collected on to the Inland Revenue.

Income tax operating in the 94/95 fiscal year on taxable income is as follows. (Taxable income is that part remaining after allowances have been deducted).

The first £3000	is taxed at	20%
£3001−23 700	is taxed at	25%
above £23 700	is taxed at	40%

Corporation tax

This is the tax paid by companies on their profits, whether distributed as dividends or not. Corporation tax for the 94/95 fiscal year is 33 per cent with a reduced rate of 25 per cent for small companies. A small company is defined as one not exceeding a certain profit figure in a particular year.

Inheritance tax

This tax applies to property passing on death, plus the cumulative value of gifts made by the deceased in the previous seven years. Gifts made within seven years of death are subject to a tapering of the tax laibility on the value of the gifts.

This tax applies to:

(a) gifts between individuals within seven years of death
(b) the transfer of property on a person's death
(c) gifts to certain trusts

For the 94/95 tax year the rates are as shown below:

Inheritance tax at death
The first £150 000 is free of tax
above   £150 000 is charged at 40%

Chargeable lifetime transfers are initially taxed at 20 per cent. Certain transfers of wealth are exempt from inheritance tax:

(a) transfers between husband and wife
(b) gifts to charities
(c) gifts to political parties and certain national bodies
(d) lifetime gifts up to a certain figure

Capital gains tax

This is a tax levied on a person or a company in respect of any asset disposed of within the fiscal year, upon which chargeable gains accrue. For instance, if a person bought an area of land as an investment and later sold it at a profit, the tax would be calculated on the profit or gain made. The rate charged is that paid on the top slice of income, i.e. the highest rate of income tax paid by an individual. Tax is liable on the following assets:

(a) investments such as antiques, jewellery, buildings, land etc.
(b) any property produced by the person disposing of it, for example works of art
(c) any currency other than sterling

The following assets are exempt:

(a) a person's main place of residence
(b) national savings certificates and Save As You Earn (SAYE) etc.
(c) wins from betting, including football pools and premium bonds
(d) compensation paid to a person for any wrong or injury incurred
(e) life assurance policies and annuities
(f) donations to charities
(g) tangible movable property with a life less than 50 years
(h) the first £5800 of your net gains
(i) private motor cars
(j) chattels sold for less than £3000

The chargeable gain is computed by totalling all the gains for the year and deducting all the losses.

Advantages of direct taxation

There are three main advantages:

(a) It is relatively cheap to collect, which results in a fairly small proportion of the income derived being used up in the collection costs.
(b) As it is administered in the United Kingdom at present it is a progressive tax, so that the lower income groups pay little or no tax, whereas the higher income groups pay progressively more. This helps to more fairly distribute spendable income.
(c) Government can determine, with a fair degree of accuracy, what level of tax income is needed, and adjust income tax rates accordingly.

Disadvantages of direct taxation

The major disadvantage is that all forms of direct taxation can be said to act as a disincentive to those being taxed. An individual may be reluctant to work overtime, because much of the extra earned will be deducted in tax. It is possible that workers whose basic wages place them in the lowest or standard tax rate find that the additional income from working extra hours put them into the highest tax range, so giving an even greater disincentive.

Relatively high corporation tax can result in many companies' finding ways of avoiding the showing of large profits. They may therefore reinvest in new plant and machinery, firm's cars or other commodities that will reduce the tax bill.

Indirect taxation

This tax applies when goods or services are paid for. It operates generally by an amount being added on to the selling price, and this addition then goes to government in the form of tax.

Value added tax (VAT)

This is a tax charged on many goods supplied by businesses. In 1994 the standard rate of tax is 17.5 per cent. In a particular VAT accounting period, usually three months, the businessman determines the output tax, i.e. the tax on the produce sold, and deducts from this the input tax, which is the tax that the business has paid on goods it has bought in. Computing in this manner ensures that it is truly a tax on the added value of the goods.

For example, a businessman might calculate the figures shown in Table 16.2.

A particular commodity may go through many stages of production and several stages of selling, each involving a different business at each stage. Tax at the current rate will be added to the gain in value of the article at each of these stages.

Certain goods are zero rated. This means that no tax is charged on these particular goods when supplied, but any input tax paid on goods or services necessary for their manufacture can be deducted.

The calculation of VAT within the construction industry is quite complex: some work is zero rated whilst the majority is standard rated at 17.5 per cent.

Zero rated work includes the following:

(a) the construction of a new self-contained dwelling
(b) the necessary civil engineering works associated with (a) above
(c) children's homes
(d) specialised retirement homes

Table 16.2

Total outputs	200 000	
VAT @ 17.5%		35 000
Total inputs	100 000	
VAT already paid @ 17.5%		17 500
VAT payable		£17 500

(e) hospices

(f) other communal living accommodation which is the main residence for at least 90 per cent of its residents

(g) buildings constructed by charities for non-business use

Standard rated work consists of any of the work not covered above, e.g. all maintenance work, new work to industrial and commercial premises, new work on hospitals, prisons and hotels etc.

A contractor who builds work which is mostly zero rated can expect a refund from the VAT authorities each period as he can reclaim the VAT already paid on the goods bought in.

Other examples of zero-rated goods are: food, books, transport, large caravans and houseboats, drugs and medicines, exports, children's clothing and footwear.

Some goods and services are exempt from VAT, which means that like zero-rated goods no tax is chargeable on their sale. But unlike zero-rated goods, input taxes paid out on purchases cannot be reclaimed. As these taxes cannot be reclaimed, the costs are ultimately passed on to the consumer. The following are examples of exempt goods: land generally, insurance, education, banking, betting charges, postal services, charges for private health treatment, trade union and professional bodies membership charges.

Businesses with a turnover of less than £45 000 per annum are not legally required to register for VAT. This means that they still pay VAT where applicable on their purchases, but this cannot be reclaimed if they are not registered.

Vehicle excise duty

This is a tax payable for all motorised vehicles used on the roads. If any vehicle is used or even parked on the public highway, a current tax disc should be displayed. Some examples of 1994 rates are:

• motor cycles less than 150 c.c.	£10 p.a.
• private cars	£130 p.a.
• light goods vehicles	£130 p.a.
• some heavy goods vehicles can cost up to	£5000 p.a.

Customs and excise duties

On many goods a duty or tax is payable before VAT is chargeable. This applies to such items as tobacco, wines, spirits, perfume and petrol. Certain imported goods are subject to customs tariffs, which can be imposed to make imported goods more expensive to purchase than home-produced goods. Some examples of duties charged during 1994 are:

• beer	12p per litre
• wine	from £1.30 to £2.20 per litre
• spirits	approximately £7.50 per litre

- cigarettes   approximately 66p per pack of 20
- cigars   £77.60 per kg
- pipe tobacco   £34.26 per kg
- leaded petrol   33.5p per litre
- unleaded petrol   28.75p per litre.

Airport taxes

This was a new addition to the taxation scene which was announced in the November budget of 1993. It imposes a tax of £5 on all departures from United Kingdom airports to destinations within Europe. Those flying to elsewhere in the world pay a £10 tax.

Advantages of indirect taxation

(a) It does not act as a disincentive to work as many taxes, particularly excise duties and VAT, are often paid without people realising it, for the tax is included in the final retail price of the good.

(b) It has been said that government can regulate the consumption of certain goods by the level of taxes imposed; this applies particularly to alcoholic drinks and tobacco. Whether or not the imposition of a high tax on these goods does have a beneficial effect on society in general is a matter of opinion, for it would be very difficult to prove such a statement. It should not be forgotten that these commodities are relatively inelastic in demand, therefore it is doubtful whether demand will fall greatly as the tax is increased.

(c) Import tariffs can help protect home industries against fierce, often subsidised, competition from abroad.

Subsidies and grants paid in Britain

In order to further the government's aim of redistribution of wealth, subsidies can be given on certain goods as discussed in Chapter 6. This means that instead of an item costing its true market price of say £1, if the government gives a subsidy of 30p per item, the consumer will now only pay 70p.

Besides direct subsidies on goods, government pays certain subsidies to industry in some circumstances, in order to further particular government objectives as described below.

To directly encourage employment

(a) *Business start-up scheme.* This is designed to provide help for those who wish to set up their own business. The scheme offers advice and financial assistance.

(b) *The long-term unemployed.* Employers who take on employees who have been out of work for at least two years receive a one-year subsidy based on the benefit payments which would otherwise have been paid by government.

(c) *Enterprise allowance scheme.* This scheme is designed to provide help during the first 12 months when a person starts to work for himself. It is intended to help unemployed people who have a business venture in mind, but who may not have the financial backing to carry themselves over the initial set-up period. People 18−65 are eligible, but must have some money of their own to invest.

(d) *Employment in development areas.* Employment prospects in development areas can be enhanced by the granting of Regional Development Grants. These grants are given for new buildings or machinery used in connection with industry. The Grant given by government is of the order of 15−20 per cent subject to certain minimum costs and eligibilities.

The encouragement of food production

Government has for many years subsidised certain forms of agriculture, and there are several reasons for this:

(a) Farmers are subject to the vagaries of the weather; varying yields of harvests and hence varying income can play havoc with a farmer's investment programme. In the past a minimum price or intervention system was mostly used, which ensured the farmers had a guaranteed minimum price for their produce. The problem with this system is that it can lead to large stockpiles of goods which are very expensive to hold. Recently there has been a move within the Common Agricultural Policy (CAP) away from high final intervention prices. Financial help is now tending to concentrate on the production stage rather than the final product selling stage.

(b) In the past, the idea of self-sufficiency has been encouraged, particularly in times of war. By giving subsidies on foods that the government wanted produced, farmers would be encouraged to change over to production of these commodities.

(c) In order to cut down on imports, and so aid the balance of payments, the growth of certain commodities has been encouraged. An example of this is sugar beet production.

Types of government aid paid to farmers

There have been many different types of subsidies and grants paid to farmers in the past, but a few operating during 1993−94 are as follows:

(a) *The farm capital grant scheme.* This allows for grants to be paid to farmers for capital expenditure over a wide range of projects, including; land drainage, permanent plant and equipment, water supply, roads, farm buildings etc. The general rate of grant is of the order of 10−20 per cent, but for farmers in less favoured areas a higher rate is payable.

(b) *The hill livestock compensatory allowance.* Under this scheme, the government gives a compensating allowance to farmers for the breeding and rearing of sheep and cattle in less favoured areas.

(c) *Environmentally sensitive areas (ESA) scheme.* Two specialist types of grants are available within these areas. Under the agreed management scheme for ESAs, within the designated areas farmers are given grants in return for agreeing to manage the land in an environmentally beneficial way.

- By not ploughing up grassland
- By not altering existing drainage systems
- By not using fungicides, insecticides or lime
- By restricting the spreading of fertilisers
- By maintaining existing lakes, reedbeds, hedges, trees and watercourses

Where work is to be carried out in an ESA to restore land to its natural condition, e.g. restoring hedges, pools, reedbeds etc. grants may be available under the conservation plan capital works.

(d) *Arable area payments (set-aside scheme).* During the mid-1990s intervention support prices paid to farmers for cereals are being reduced. In order to offset the decrease in farm incomes and also to encourage farmers to reduce production of these crops this scheme has been developed. It allows farmers to leave fields that were producing certain crops to return to natural grass cover. In return farmers will be paid a grant depending upon the crop previously grown.

(e) *Price guarantees in respect of the EEC common agricultural policy.* Support buying, or intervention buying, is a system operated usually through marketing boards, whereby when the normal market price of a commodity falls below the intervention price the board will buy the surplus at an agreed figure. The goods are then held in storage until the market price rises and the surplus can be sold on the open market. This system has two advantages, it provides the farmer with a guaranteed price, but it also has the effect of removing the surplus goods from the market, thus ensuring higher prices return quicker.

Criticisms of the intervention price system are firstly that high intervention prices lead to high prices in the shops. Secondly large stockpiles can come into being which in practice are not sold off. They are either stored for long periods which is expensive, or given away to needy causes. The third criticism is that high intervention prices encourage farmers to produce goods already in surplus.

In order to reduce these problems the emphasis of farm subsidies is now moving towards subsidies during production, rather than the government agreeing to buy at relatively high prices. This allows more of a market situation to exist, as the goods are sold at market price, not at or above intervention price.

Social benefits paid to individuals

The information contained within this chapter has concentrated on the government income-gathering systems — taxation, and the grants or subsidies affecting business or the balance of payments.

There are many benefits paid out by government to individuals, e.g.

- state pensions
- sick pay
- child care allowance
- unemployment benefit etc.

The details of these many and varied schemes will not be discussed here.

Questions

1 Find out the current levels of direct and indirect taxation operating at present within Britain.
2 What are the main fiscal policies being followed by government at the present time. Why are these policies being operated, and are they working?
3 Discuss the implications of changing Britain's tax system over to a wholly indirect system.

Chapter 17

Monetary control in Britain

Origins and functions of money

When the various civilisations began to develop, trading between nations became somewhat of a problem. From the earliest times, trading had existed, but was based on a system of bartering, whereby goods were directly exchanged with other goods. At times this form of exchange was very impractical, particularly when one tried to swap a large item for a selection of smaller ones.

It then became necessary to have an intermediate medium of exchange. It was also necessary to have this money, as this is what it was, in a durable form, so that it could be stored to enable large items to be saved for. By valuing goods in terms of the particular money concerned, it was possible to compare values of goods. It was also necessary that contracts could be entered into, with the knowledge that when payment was made in the future, the money payment would be of a known value.

The four functions of money are therefore:

(a) a medium of exchange
(b) a store of value, or wealth
(c) a measure of value
(d) a standard of deferred payment

In order that money should fulfil these functions, it should possess the following properties:

(a) Its main quality should be acceptability. All people likely to come into contact with the money, should accept it at its understood value.

(b) The money should be portable. It would be ridiculous having bricks as a form of money, for they would make large holes in one's pockets.

(c) Durability is another important quality; perishable foods, for instance, would be useless as money as they would not last long. Paper money used today is not very durable, and because of this, it constantly has to be replaced, which is an expensive operation. It was for this reason that the £1 coin was introduced into the coinage system.

(d) Money should be capable of being divided into the smallest divisions likely to be required. Television sets could not be used as money, for they could not be divided into usable smaller segments.

(e) Money should be scarce enough to give it the required value. In Britain, fir cones could not be used as money, for anyone could go out in the autumn, and collect lorry loads free.

(f) It should be difficult to imitate or forge. If forgery were easy, this would lead to large-scale criminal activities which could upset the whole monetary system.

(g) All items that are used as money must be homogeneous, that is they must be of the same material, and of the same size, so that each can be seen to have the same value.

In the past, many commodities have been used as media of exchange, but generally they failed to possess one or more of the above properties, and so eventually they went out of fashion. They have now been replaced with coinage systems. Some examples of old media of exchange are: cowrie shells; cigarettes and nylon stockings during the last war; even cattle have been used at certain times.

Modern 'real' money generally consists in cash form of metal coins or paper notes. Original coins were minted out of gold, and the printing of paper money was allowed only when the value of the notes was backed by an equivalent value of gold bullion. The banknote issue since 1939 has not been backed by gold and is now known as a fiduciary issue. Today, as silver and gold have become scarcer, and also because these metals are not too durable, they are no longer used in coins in current circulation.

Prior to 1920 'silver' coins consisted of 0.925 fine silver. In 1920, however, this was reduced to 0.500 fine silver, and in 1947 coins were minted of a copper nickel alloy which contained no silver at all.

Cash in the form of notes and coin is essential for small personal transactions, but to carry around large sums would be inconvenient, and would encourage crime. Various means of paying money from one person to another have evolved to overcome this problem.

A bank cheque

This is an instruction, signed and dated, given by person A to person B, instructing A's bank to pay from A's account, to B or B's account, a certain amount of money. Cheques are valid only if presented within six months of the signing date. In theory, cheques can be written on anything, but in practice, to facilitate mechanical checking they are standardised, with the bank's branch sorting code and customer's code imprinted on them. It must be remembered that a cheque itself is not money, for it is not legal tender, although it can be passed on to a third person, if properly countersigned. It is only an instruction to transfer a deposit, which must already exist, from one account to another.

Direct debit

This is a process whereby a creditor can make a direct claim on a customer's bank account. Approval is given for this by the customer signing an appropriate form. By using this system, single or multiple transfers (standing orders), for example mortgage repayments, can be facilitated. The whole system of direct debiting and credit transfer is also known as the bank giro system.

Bank draft

This is really a form of cheque which, instead of being drawn on a customer's account, is drawn on the bank. A bank draft is therefore considered to be less of a financial risk than the acceptance of a cheque drawn on a customer's account where there is always the chance that it will not be honoured.

Credit cards

These are cards issued by banks to creditworthy customers, enabling these customers to obtain goods or services on credit, up to a predetermined limit. The goods can either be paid for next month, in which case little or generally no interest is payable, or be paid for over several months. Interest a little above that paid for a normal overdraft is payable for this service.

Access, Barclaycard, are examples of credit cards in wide use.

Bill of exchange

This can be defined as 'an unconditional order in writing, addressed by one person to another, signed by the person giving it, requiring the person to whom it is addressed to pay on demand or at a stated future date a sum of money to a certain person, or to the order of that person, or bearer'.

Bills of exchange are used widely in international trade, and they are used as follows.

A supplier agrees to accept payment for goods by a bill of exchange. He then writes out a bill, stating his address, the customer's name and address, the date, the amount in writing and in figures, and the date the bill becomes due. He then signs it and sends it to the customer. The customer signs it as accepted, and states the bank at which it is payable. The bill is then classed as an accepted bill, and the supplier has three alternative courses of action:

(a) The bill can be held until it falls due for payment, and the payment made as directed on the bill.

(b) The bill can be endorsed to be made over to someone else.
(c) The bill can be discounted at a bank or more usually a discount house. This involves receiving a slightly lower value for the bill, but there is the advantage that payment is received immediately. The discount house then holds the bill and receives payment when due.

Treasury bills are means used by government to finance the Public Sector Borrowing Requirement (PSBR). They are usually for three months, and are offered for tender each Friday, to the discount houses. They are payable in full (current values of bills offered are £5000, £10 000, £25 000, £50 000, £100 000, and £250 000), therefore the tender figure offered is lower than the face value.

Electronic funds transfer at the point of sale (EFTPOS)

This system is operated by using a card similar to a credit card issued to a customer by the bank operating the customer's account. When goods are purchased at participating outlets the card is put through a machine and the money is automatically taken out of the customer's account immediately.

Control of the money supply

Only about one-fifth of the so-called money supply is in the form of notes and coin, the rest is in the form of 'bank' money, or 'created' money, which is formed by the normal transactions of banking.

In the day-to-day running of a bank, it was soon discovered that not everyone who had deposited money with the bank wanted their money out at the same time. This meant that, providing the bank kept enough money in reserve for customer withdrawals in the form of cash, the rest could be loaned out at a favourable rate of interest. At present banks are required to hold a certain small percentage of their liabilities in the form of cash or deposits. In very simple terms, the rate is 5 per cent, this means that if the bank receives from a customer a £1000 deposit this can form 5 per cent of secured money, and the bank can lend out £19 000 to another customer.

In Chapter 15, monetarism was discussed. The operation of this policy hinges on the ability to control the money supply, or more specifically the amount of money 'created' by banks. This is done in various ways.

1. By increasing the bank base rates.   This makes interest rates generally much higher, and people are reluctant to take out loans, therefore in theory the money supply shrinks. In practice, this may work with private individuals, but businesses are committed to try to continue in business, and during such periods when the government takes these actions, many businesses find that they require loans, often termed distress loans, to help them ride out the recession. Certain types of loans then are more likely to increase, rather than decrease during such periods, which makes the policy less effective.

2. Special deposits. In order to decrease a bank's lending power, the Bank of England can insist on special deposits, calculated as a percentage of total eligible liabilities, being deposited with the Bank of England. This has the effect of reducing a bank's reserve assets, so that less money can now be loaned to customers, whilst still maintaining the 5 per cent reserve assets ratio. Special deposits bear an interest payable to the depositing bank, but at certain times the Bank of England can insist on supplementary special deposits being lodged with it, which do not bear interest.

In the operation of a strict monetary policy, the Bank of England is likely to instigate other measures:

(a) It will give guidance to commercial banks on their method of lending, stating where preferences should be given when considering loans. Generally priorities are given to exporting or depressed manufacturing industry first. Construction is not usually regarded as a top priority case.

(b) The amount of money in general circulation can be reduced somewhat, by the Bank of England selling off government stocks, more usually known as gilt-edged stocks. As people buy these stocks, then the money in circulation declines, and it is hoped that this results in a slowing down of inflation.

Because of the existence of many different kinds of so-called money today, in the UK, different definitions have been evolved as follows:

- M_0 Consists of notes and coin in circulation outside the Bank of England together with bankers' deposits with the Bank of England.
- M_1 This consists of notes and coin, and current accounts at banks. This is known as the narrow definition of money, and is money in its most liquid form, which can be used to settle debts immediately.
- M_2 This is a term not now used by official UK statistics, but nevertheless, this definition gives a slightly broader description of the money supply, as it consists of M_1 plus deposit accounts in banks.
- M_3 This gives the broadest description of the money supply, for it includes M_2 plus all other deposits held in the UK in the form of foreign currency, national savings etc.
- M_4 Consists of M_3 plus building society deposits.

The Bank of England

This is the centre point of the whole British monetary system, and as such is often referred to as the Central Bank.

Although it does deal with a few private customers, the main activities of the bank are concerned with the carrying out of national policies and national and international banking transactions.

The main functions of the bank are described below.

Banker to the government

The bank looks after the income from taxation, takes care of payments, and also manages the national debt. Loans are raised, mainly by the selling of short-term treasury bills, and by the issue of new long-term government stocks.

The accounts of many government departments are also held at the bank. Many activities are carried out as a service to government, by implementing various policies as described earlier. The bank also acts as Britain's link with international monetary bodies, as it helps to protect the value of the exchange rate, and also deals with the International Monetary Fund.

Banker to the commercial banks

A certain amount of reserves have to be deposited with the central bank, and this can be used to help regulate the monetary supply.

The daily working of the banking system means that by the paying and receiving of cheques, a bank may owe money to another bank, or vice versa, at the end of the day's dealings. These transactions can be balanced by drawing on, or paying into, the various banks' reserves at the central bank.

Controller of the issue of notes and coin

The bank is the sole supplier of notes in England, and new notes are issued either in return for old, or when backed by a new issue of securities.

The lender of last resort

Discount houses, as mentioned earlier, discount bills of exchange. In order to do this they borrow money, generally for very short periods, from commercial banks who may have a surplus of funds for a day or two, or from large companies in industry. The money which is borrowed is likely to be recalled at very short notice, and as the Bills of Exchange are not immediately cashable, except at a discount, the discount houses can find themselves temporarily short of funds at certain times. It is at these times that the Bank of England acts as lender of last resort to the discount houses, by lending money to them at what used to be the minimum lending rate.

Questions

1 Discuss the role of the Bank of England:
   (a) in respect of implementing government policy
   (b) in respect of daily banking activities
2 Why is it so difficult to define the meaning of money?
3 Discuss, with the aid of an example, how a fast flow of money in the economy can stimulate economic growth.

Chapter 18

International trade

Advantages of international trade

When confronted with newspaper headlines containing such phrases as balance of payments, export drives, and import restrictions, many people ask the question, 'Why do we need to trade with other countries? Would it not be better to produce everything ourselves?'

This chapter discusses the factors affecting the operation of international trade, and it is hoped that by the end of this section, the answers to the above questions will be obvious.

The two main reasons why it is advantageous to practice international trade are set out below.

Inability to produce goods nationally

In all countries, there are certain commodities that cannot be home produced. This may be due to:

(a) Climatic reasons affecting the growth of crops, e.g. Britain cannot grow bananas or oranges, except in carefully controlled conditions.
(b) The total lack of certain minerals and other types of natural resources within the boundaries of a particular country, or the existence of these commodities in very limited quantities, e.g.
    (i) Many nations rely on the Middle East countries for supplies of oil.
    (ii) Japan has to import iron ore for its developing steel industry, from Australia.

(iii) South Africa produces three quarters of the world's gold supply, many countries have to obtain their quantities of gold from this source.

International division of labour

Earlier in the book, the advantages of division of labour within a business or industry were discussed.

The theory of division of labour can be extended internationally, so that it can be seen that particular countries become very expert and efficient at producing certain goods. For example, in Britain by expending 1000 units of resources (a certain mix of the factors of production), either 400 units of pottery or 50 cars could be produced. In Japan, the same 1000 units of resources could produce 300 units of pottery, or 60 cars. If in each country, 10 000 units of resources were available for the manufacture of pottery and cars, and each country used 50 per cent of their resources for the production of each commodity, the result would be as shown in Table 18.1.

If, instead of the above situation, each country concentrated on producing the commodity which it could produce the most efficiently, then the result would be as shown in Table 18.2.

It can be seen from Table 18.2 that the totals jointly produced are better

Table 18.1

	Production			
	Pottery		Cars	
	Resources used	Units made	Resources used	Units made
Britain	5 000	2000	5 000	250
Japan	5 000	1500	5 000	300
Totals	10 000	3500	10 000	550

Table 18.2

	Production			
	Pottery		Cars	
	Resources used	Units made	Resources used	Units made
Britain	10 000	4000	—	—
Japan	—	—	10 000	600
Totals	10 000	4000	10 000	600

than before, so that if now an exchange can take place, so that Britain exports pottery to Japan, and Japan exports cars to Britain, then both countries will be better off.

Consider now another situation. For 1000 units of resources in Britain, the same quantity of pottery, 400 units, can be produced, or 200 bicycles. In Japan, for 1000 units of resources, 300 units of pottery, or 100 bicycles could be produced. In this situation Britain can produce both items more efficiently than Japan. Firstly, however, consider Table 18.3, which shows the production of 10 000 units of resources in each country, again equally divided between the two products. This gives total production for the two countries of 3500 units of pottery and 1500 bicycles.

Even though Britain produces both items more efficiently, it has the greatest relative production advantage when making bicycles, where it is twice as efficient as Japan. In the production of pottery, it is only $1\frac{1}{3}$ times as efficient. Japan then could be said to be less inefficient in the production of pottery, and so it might concentrate all its resources on this commodity. This however would only produce 3000 units. Britain would be best advised to concentrate the majority of its production on bicycles, just allowing say 20 per cent of its resources to be used to produce pottery, which will augment Japan's output. The result shown in Table 18.4, is that when countries concentrate their

Table 18.3

	Production			
	Pottery		Bicycles	
	Resources used	Units made	Resources used	Units made
Britain	5 000	2000	5 000	1000
Japan	5 000	1500	5 000	500
Totals	10 000	3500	10 000	1500

Table 18.4

	Production			
	Pottery		Bicycles	
	Resources used	Units made	Resources used	Units made
Britain	2 000	800	8000	1600
Japan	10 000	3000	—	—
Totals	12 000	3800	8000	1600

production on the commodities in which they have the greatest comparative advantage, then the overall production totals will be greater. This idea forms the basis of the law of comparative advantage.

By the operation of international trade it can be seen that the world as a whole gains more benefit if countries trade with one another. Also, by the action of trade, many countries are brought into close negotiation with each other, which in time leads to greater co-operation and less conflict.

The advantages of international trade, as detailed above, rely on certain assumptions that are not valid in practice.

(a) It assumes that there is low unemployment in all the participating countries. Problems arise where a country has high unemployment, but still continues to buy many goods from abroad. The government must ask itself whether this is a good thing, or whether they should try to curtail imports, in the hope of stimulating home industries.

(b) International trade, in its simplest and most advantageous form, does not cater for tariffs or quotas. These, when operated, restrict the operation of international trade.

(c) Broadly speaking, in order to trade with other countries, in the long term, trade has to be two ways, or better still, between many countries. If trade continued on a one-way basis for a long period, then currency problems would arise (see later sections).

Disadvantages of international trade

It has been shown that in many ways international trade is advantageous. There are, however, certain situations where governments take steps to prevent trading taking place.

(a) In the past, in Britain, government has in times of war sought to make the country as self-sufficient as possible in terms of food.

(b) When two countries have broken off diplomatic relations then the government of one or both countries may pass legislation to prevent trading between the countries, e.g. Rhodesia (Zimbabwe) in the late 1970s.

(c) When a developing new industry is struggling in a particular country by reason of overseas competition, then it is possible to build up a strong home market, by preventing the importing of the competing goods. Without this protection of new industries, they may not develop the scale of operations necessary to make them financially viable. This is particularly true of highly capital-intensive industries.

(d) When a country has a high unemployment rate, and especially when certain industries are threatened by cheap imports, then the population may bring pressure to bear on the government, to impose restrictions.

Restrictions on international trade

These can be imposed in several ways.

1. Tariffs.   This is simply the operation of a system of taxes, such as customs' duties on imported tobacco, wines and spirits.

The main function of a tariff is to increase the price at which imported goods are sold, and so make home-produced goods more attractive, from a cost point of view, to the consumers.

2. Quotas.   With this method of restriction, the number of imported units of a particular commodity which are allowed to enter the country is regulated. Such a system is operated, for example, by a country limiting the number of cars being imported, to allow the domestic car industry to enjoy a larger home market. Quotas are sometimes operated on total value of goods, rather than number of items.

3. Embargoes.   At certain times, the government may refuse to allow the importing of any units of a particular commodity, or it may ban the trading altogether, with certain countries.

Whilst trying to restrict imports into a country, government often tries to increase exports. In practice, the two are often not compatible. Whatever type of restriction is imposed, it might ultimately lead to other countries, who can no longer export so much, imposing retaliatory restrictions on imports from the restricting country.

Balance of payments

A country has to operate its international trading activities like an ordinary business. As in an ordinary business, goods have to be bought in to be sold, and it is necessary to sell goods, in order to obtain money to buy more goods. Similarly, Britain has to export goods, in order to earn the foreign currency with which to buy goods from overseas. In a business, the transactions are noted down, and periodically a balance sheet is produced which will show the state of finances. Similarly, with a country, a balance sheet is produced annually, to show the state of the country's international financial dealings.

Consider Table 18.5, which is a simplified version of Britain's balance of payments for 1982, 1988 and 1991, which has been taken from the annual abstract of statistics.

Visible trade consists of balancing visible imports against visible exports. A negative figure indicates that import payments are greater than export receipts. Visible goods are those goods which are actually transported. Britain often has a negative balance on visible goods transactions.

Table 18.5   UK Balance of Payments for 1987 1988 and 1991 in £ millions

	1982	*1988*	*1991*
Current a/c			
Visible trade	1 911	− 21 480	− 10 290
Invisible trade	2 741	5 302	3 969
Current balance	4 652	− 16 178	− 6 321
Assets & liabilities a/c			
Investment transactions	− 8 640	− 4 613	− 12 497
Currency transactions	3 855	14 398	8 207
Overseas banking	409	− 315	9 338
Official reserves	1 421	− 2 761	− 2 662
Other asset & liab. movemts.	435	2 689	2 863
Balance of capital a/c	− 2 520	9 398	5 249
Balancing item	− 2 132	6 780	1 072
Balancing item + capital a/c	− 4 652	16 178	6 321

Source: Annual Abstract of Statistics 1993

Invisible trade is the value of work transacted in the services field, and includes such activities as shipping, insurance and money spent by tourists. A positive figure indicates greater exporting of these services than importing. Generally Britain has a positive balance on invisibles.

The visible and invisible trading balances make up the current account. The capital account shows the position with respect to the flow of money, other than that used in trading activities covered by the current account. Capital is moved from one country to another, for one of three reasons:

(a) As a loan or gift from one country to another. For instance, if Britain loaned £2 million to a foreign country, this would be shown as a debit, or negative figure on the balance sheet. Conversely if America loaned £10 million to Britain, this would be a credit or positive entry in the balance sheet.

(b) In order to invest money in businesses in foreign countries. For example, if a British company invested £2 million in a car assembly plant abroad, then this would be shown as a debit, for the money is going out of the country. The profits or interest gained on the overseas investment, providing it came back into Britain is a credit, under invisible trade. British banks often make international loans, a loan from a British bank to one overseas would be shown as a debit.

(c) When countries are threatened with war, or other major political problems, many people try to leave, together with as much wealth as they can legally, or illegally take with them. They invest their wealth in another trouble-free country, in order to keep it safe.

The capital account transactions consist of several types of transactions. Investment and currency operations are carried out during normal trading activities. The other types of capital movement are more usually involved in balancing the country's international trading account. These consist of borrowings or repayments between banks of different countries. Drawings on, or additions to, official reserves refers to the decreases or increases in the reserves of foreign currency or gold held by the Bank of England. Drawings on reserves are shown as a + whilst additions are shown as −.

The last group of transactions involve movements of funds concerning assets or liabilities of non-bank private and public corporations and general government.

Table 18.5 has two main balances: the current balance and the capital account balance. The capital account balance includes those actions necessary to balance the overall trading position as described above and so the two balances should correspond. Due to statistical errors in the compilation of the accounts they are rarely the same and so a balancing item is included to correct for this.

Balancing the current account

From Table 18.5 it can be seen that the visible trade shows negative figures for 1988 and 1991. This means that a greater value of goods was imported than exported. The reasons for this imbalance revolve around the law of supply and demand. There is less demand for British goods overseas than there is for foreign goods in Britain.

Consumers often base their decisions on three factors: cost, quality and availability. All of these factors can be affected by the manufacturers but cost can also be changed by government policies. In order to reduce the volume of imported goods tarrifs would effectively increase the cost of imports, making home-produced goods appear relatively cheaper. Many goods imported into Britain are considerably cheaper than those manufactured in Britain. These goods are produced by countries with much lower labour costs. For instance many items of clothing are imported from China, Korea, Taiwan or Portugal. As economies develop in these countries labour rates will eventually rise so that costs may become comparable.

There are two other methods by which a government can improve the current account.

1. Deflationary techniques. If inflation was to increase in Britain at a higher rate than in other countries, then eventually Britain's goods would become relatively more expensive than those in other countries, and so exports would fall. At the same time, foreign goods imported into Britain would become relatively cheaper than home-produced goods. It can be seen that this would lead to a bad balance of visible trade. It should be remembered that in this context the level of inflation is important only when related to other countries. The fact that Britain might have 20 per cent inflation could be an advantage, at least to our balance of payments, if the rest of the world has 30 per cent.

Deflationary measures are carried out then, to try to bring inflation under control, and to improve trade. These measures generally involve cutting back on demand in home markets, either by fiscal or monetary methods, in order to cut home demand which will reduce imports, and also encourage manufacturers to export.

2. Devaluation and exchange rates. Until 1972, the value of the £ was fixed or pegged, against other currencies at a fixed value. When a country has a fixed exchange rate, then it is possible to devalue its currency in terms of other currencies. For example, prior to 1967 the £ was valued at $2.8. In 1967 the £ was devalued, so that it was now valued at $2.4. Prior to 1967, a car valued at £10 000 in Britain would have cost $28 000 in America; after devaluation, it would have cost only $24 000. Thus devaluation tends to encourage exports as British goods now appear cheaper in America. By the same token, before devaluation, a car selling for $14 000 in America would cost £5000 in Britain. After devaluation the same car would now cost £5833. Devaluation, therefore also tends to discourage imports.

Floating exchange rates and the exchange rate mechanism (ERM)

There are many problems with the adoption of a fixed rate. It means that there are often times when devaluation is thought necessary, due to imbalances of trade, and this not only causes sudden jumps in worldwide currency values and trading possibilities, but also problems of people speculating on possible devaluations, by hoarding vast sums of currency in the hope of making a profit when values change.

In 1972, Britain 'floated' the £, and in 1973/74 all other major currencies did likewise. A floating currency is where the value is not fixed against others, but varies in response to the supply and demand conditions of the currency concerned. Consider Fig. 18.1, which shows the actual workings of international trade and payments. The problem of dealing internationally is that each country has its own currency. A British importer, for example, cannot pay an American exporter directly in pounds, for they would be useless in America. Each payment transaction therefore has to pass through the foreign exchange market, which in practice comprises the foreign exchange departments of banks in many countries. Consider the top trading transaction of Fig. 18.1. Goods are exported from Britain to America. The final consumers in America pass on their dollars eventually to the American importer, who pays them into his bank. His bank then deals with the payment on paper, via the exchange market to the British exporter's bank. At this point the currency is changed from dollars to pounds, at the rate operating at that time. The payment then is credited to the British exporter's bank in pounds, the British exporter then paying the British manufacturer in pounds.

Consider now the bottom trading path (Fig. 18.1). Goods are exported from

213

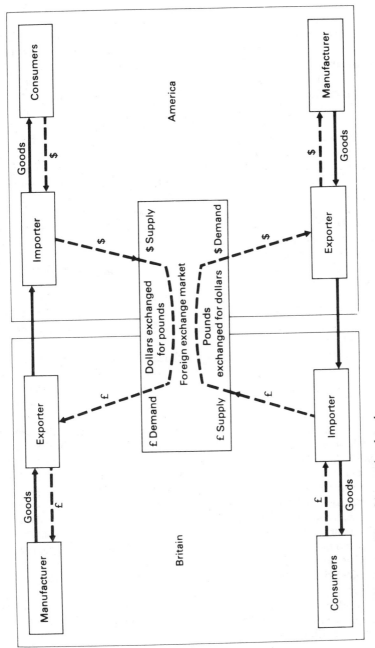

Fig. 18.1 The working of international trade

America to Britain and payment is made in a similar manner to that previously, but in reverse. At this point the workings of the foreign exchange market and the rates of exchange can now be studied in more depth.

The foreign exchange market gets the pounds to pay the British exporter, in practice from the British importer, who pays pounds into the system. Similarly, there is a through flow of dollars, from American consumers paying American importers who pay into the market, the dollars finding their way to the American exporters then to the manufacturers. It is obvious therefore that in the long period, in order for a country to export, it must also import, and vice versa, in order for currency exchange to operate.

Another way of looking at this is to say that exporters build up at their banks reserves of foreign currency which in fact are only promises to pay. These promises are then exchanged for the British promises to pay. The supply and demand of the value of these promises gives the exchange rate. For example, if there were relatively few dollar promises being exchanged for relatively many pound promises, then the value of the dollar would rise in terms of pounds. This might correspond to an exchange rate of say $2.35 to the £ if previously the exchange rate was $2.4 to the £. In the reverse situation, where relatively many dollar promises were chasing relatively few pound promises, then the value of the pound would rise in relation to the dollar to a figure of say $2.45 to the £.

In order that transactions can take place when a country does not have any currency reserves, either because they are all used up, or it never had any, the country has to actually buy or borrow foreign currency; this can be seen in Table 18.5.

A floating exchange rate is where the market forces of supply and demand are allowed to result in an equilibrium exchange rate. At the present time, however, governments with this method of rate determination often intervene to alter the rate. For example, the value of the pound would fall if there were relatively many pounds chasing too few dollars. This situation might occur where Britain had high imports and low exports with America, whilst America would have low imports and high exports with Britain. Within the foreign exchange 'box' of Fig. 18.1, many pounds would be entering, whilst many dollars would be extracted. The Bank of England, at such times, buys pounds on the foreign exchange market with its reserves of dollars; this operation increases the number of dollars, and so the value of the dollar drops. When the value of the pound gets too high, the reverse operation is carried out. By carrying out these transactions, the short-term fluctuations of the markets can be ironed out, and the value of the exchange rate is kept steadier than it would otherwise have been.

In 1989 Britain joined the European monetary system (EMS). The eventual objective of the EMS is a single European currency. A first step towards this was the adoption of the European currency unit (ECU) to which all member country currencies were related. The value of the ECU in relation to member countries in 1989 can be seen in Table 18.6.

When a country entered the exchange rate mechanism (ERM) its currency was given a set value against the ECU and the currency value, in ECU terms, was allowed to vary only by up to 2.25 per cent either side of the central ECU

Table 18.6 Value of national currency in relation to
the ECU in 1989

Currency	Amount of currency to 1 ECU
Deutschmark	2.07
French franc	7.02
Sterling	0.67
Italian lira	1510.66
Dutch guilder	2.30
Belgian & Luxembourg franc	43.38
Spanish peseta	130.43
Danish kroner	8.06
Irish punt	0.77
Greek drachma	206.00
Portuguese escudo	173.30

value. Initially when Britain joined it was allowed to have a 6 per cent variation.
The pound at this time was pegged within the ERM, but was free floating against
all other world currencies. This system had the advantage of the pegging
system, in that traders would know within a fairly narrow range what values
the different currencies would have. It also had the advantage of floating
exchange rates, whereby rates can vary slightly in response to market forces.
In 1992 severe pressure was put upon the ERM by aggressive dealing on the
foreign exchange market. Britain could only keep the pound within its band
by constantly buying its own currency. This appeared to put up demand for
the pound and brought it just above the lower limit of the trading band. This
could not continue for long and Britain was faced with two alternatives. Either
the pound had to be devalued in terms of the ECU, or Britain had to pull out
of the system altogether. The latter was the course chosen. At the present time
(in 1993) the pound is again freely floating against all currencies. There is
a possibility that at some future date Britain will again join the ERM. During
the summer of 1993 considerable pressure was placed on other currencies within
the ERM and after frantic discussions and negotiations it was agreed to allow
much greater fluctuation of currency values. Instead of being allowed to
fluctuate only 2.25 per cent either side of the central value they can now vary
by plus or minus 15 per cent. This virtually means that in the short/medium
term the currencies are again freely floating.

International Monetary Fund (IMF)

Ideally, each country would hope to achieve an exact balance of payments each
year. In practice this just is not possible, and the best that can be achieved
is that over the long term (several years), a balance could be obtained.

Inevitably there will be countries that have a net deficit on their balance of payments in certain years. One means of overcoming these short-term financial problems is to borrow money from other sources, one such source being the IMF.

The IMF came into being as a result of the Bretton Woods Conference in 1944, which tried to put international finances on a stable basis, by fixing fairly rigidly the value of currencies in relation to one another. It was hoped that world trade would be encouraged by this action. When Britain devalued the pound in 1967 instabilities in other currencies ensued, with the result that by 1973/74 most currencies were no longer fixed, but were floating. This continues up to the present day, and so the IMF no longer has the rigid grasp on the control of international finance that it previously enjoyed.

The IMF's main function now is to act as a source of loans for member countries in financial difficulties, and in 1978 it had 128 member countries. Each member has to pay a certain quota into the fund; originally this was paid 25 per cent in gold, and 75 per cent in the currency of that particular country. Since 1976, however, the payment in gold has not been necessary. Members are allowed to withdraw the first 25 per cent slice or 'tranche' as it is termed as of right. Each succeeding slice withdrawn, and this may take the withdrawals over the quota total, must be backed by strong assurances by the borrowing country. These usually take the form of adopting certain policies that will correct the particular financial problem. The quotas and withdrawals are valued in special drawing rights (SDR), which in practice is a currency operated by the IMF and which can easily be compared and valued in terms of other currencies. Other facilities besides the SDR loans are operated; for example, the 'General Arrangements to Borrow' is a means whereby a country can arrange a private loan from a group of ten powerful nations. 'Swap' arrangements can also be accommodated, where two countries agree to swap currencies to their mutual advantage.

During the late 1970s the importance of the IMF has declined, mainly due to the floating of exchange rates helping to alleviate balance of payment problems. One of its main activities today is to act as a forum for discussions concerning world currency and debt problems.

The European Community (EC)

There has been co-operation between European countries in certain fields for many years.

In 1952 the European Coal and Steel Community was formed to co-ordinate operations concerning the mining of coal and iron ores and the sales of these products.

The European Atomic Energy Community was set up to jointly develop policies concerning research into the use of atomic energy within the member countries.

In 1957 the Treaty of Rome was passed which resulted in the European Economic Community (EEC) formally coming into existence. In 1972 Britain joined the EEC, which at the present time (now the EC) consists of Belgium, Denmark, France, Germany, Ireland, Italy, Greece, Luxembourg, The Netherlands, Portugal, Spain and the United Kingdom.

The main objectives of the EC

The common market

The aim ultimately is for the EC to act as a common market with goods, capital and labour being freely available in and transferrable between all countries. This has been a long, slow process and is still continuing in many areas. There are many problems with trying to treat the EC as one common market:

(a) different legislation in different countries
(b) differing specifications for goods produced
(c) currency fluctuations
(d) problems of mobility of labour between countries
(e) differing government policies concerning subsidies and grants
(f) differing tarrifs on imported goods
(g) differing professional qualifications between countries

The Single European Act was signed by the member countries and came into force in July 1987. This states that the European Community is an 'area without internal frontiers in which the free movement of goods, persons, services and capital is ensured in accordance with the provisions of this treaty'. The full implementation of the Single European Act will involve much discussion and negotiation on the points noted above. Although 1992 was quoted as the date when a true single market was to come into existence, many factors are still not sorted out. In one respect, that of currency value, unity seems further away than ever after the problems of August 1993 when currencies were given wider operating bands.

The social charter

The social charter was outlined in 1989 and this charter endeavours to give common rights and privileges to workers within the member countries. Aspects covered include:

(a) freedom of movement
(b) vocational training
(c) equal treatment for men and women (the UK at present has problems with this, with the differing pension ages)
(d) protection for children, adolescents, the elderly and disabled
(e) health protection and safety at the workplace
(f) information consultation and worker participation
(g) fair remuneration in employment
(h) improvements in living and working standards

218

(i) social protection (guaranteeing of benefits)
(j) freedom of association and collective bargaining

By equalising the above factors between countries it will hopefully lead to common training practices, labour costs and employment practices generally, but more importantly a greater mobility of labour.

Many people are still asking, 'Why did we join, and what can possibly be the advantages for Britain?'

British industry during the 1960s and 1970s was suffering from ever-increasing competition from abroad. By joining the EC, it was hoped that a suitable environment could be created which would encourage businessmen to take full advantage of any economies and growth prospects in their particular industry. The advantages can be summarised as follows:

(a) There is in the EC a potential home market, five times the size of Britain's alone.
(b) Due to the larger market potential, greater use can be made in certain industries of economies of scale, particularly with reference to capital-intensive industries. This may lead to products becoming more competitive, not only within the EC but in the wider world market.
(c) By providing a stable market situation for industry, businessmen can plan further into the future without too many dramatic changes in policy.
(d) Industry can take advantage of the grants and other forms of aid given via the European Regional Development Fund, which in time will replace aid given by the British government to the development areas.

Against these advantages, however, have to be weighed the disadvantages of:

(a) the possibility of dearer food in Britain than if we had not joined
(b) the political and psychological effect on the population of losing a certain amount of its independence

Questions

1 Discuss the advantages and disadvantages of international trade.
2 Newspaper headlines have suggested that North Sea oil will be Britain's saviour, in terms of balance of payments problems. Discuss this with relevance to the long and short term.
3 From the latest annual abstract of statistics, analyse the balance of payments over the last five years. Discuss possible causes which may be relevant to particular events.
4 Why does the foreign exchange rate fluctuate?

Chapter 19

Government effects on the construction industry

Introduction

In the course of the previous chapters, various isolated references have been made to the effects of government policies on the construction industry. This is inevitable, due to the overlapping nature of the various topics being discussed. As this point is of such fundamental importance to the levels of operation of the various sectors, it was thought best to devote a chapter purely to this topic. Where there has been previous discussion on a particular point, then only a summarised note will be made.

Government policies which are relevant here can be grouped under three headings: monetary, fiscal and others.

Monetary policies

During the 1970s and 1980s one of the major problems for the construction industry was that of high interest rates; these peaked in 1992 as a result of trying to support the value of sterling in the ERM (see Chapter 18).

The controlling of the money supply by influencing interest rates affects all sectors of the industry. In times of monetary restraint, people are generally less inclined to borrow money, because of the high level of interest that will have to be paid. At the same time, high deposit account interest will encourage people to leave money in these accounts, rather than spend it.

Industrial and commercial expansion or replacement of buildings may be cut, because to go ahead and pay excessive interest on projects may outweigh any profit or economies which might accrue, particularly when output from the business in question might have to be reduced due to a depression.

Private housing is hit especially hard by a period of high interest rates, and this is one of the main reasons for the erratic movement of the new private housing line in Fig. 7.2. A high base rate inevitably leads to a high mortgage rate, for building societies find it necessary to increase their rates in order to offer attractive interest on their deposit accounts. High mortgage rates lead to a reduction in the demand for mortgages, for two reasons:

(a) The monthly repayments become too excessive for many people to cope with.

(b) The maximum that can be borrowed, based upon a person's income, is reduced, so that large advances can no longer be made.

This stagnation in house movement inevitably leads to less new homes being demanded.

Looking at house building from the supply side, speculative development necessarily involves the tying up of large sums of money, in the purchase of land, and in the erection of units ready for sale. A planned cash flow is essential, and if a phase of completed houses does not sell quickly, then much capital is tied up, on which high interest has to be paid. For this reason, speculative development of all types tends to be held back during high interest periods.

Monetary policy as such does not have any direct effect on public sector works, although it may lead to an increase in costs for the financing of contracts, which may result in certain jobs being shelved.

Fiscal policies

These do not often have a great direct effect on the industry, except possibly in two situations.

At present VAT is payable on most construction work except new housing (see Chapter 16).

Although it is difficult to find proof of this, it would be fair to assume that a considerable amount of repair work is now being done on a DIY basis in order not to pay the VAT on the labour used by a registered builder. This leads to the conclusion that maintenance work, as shown by the statistics, should be of a higher value than shown.

Prior to VAT, a tax existed on the number of employees that were employed by businesses. This was known as the Selective Employment Tax (SET), and lasted from 1966 to 1973. With this tax, manufacturing industry could claim back the tax, but service industries which included construction could not. This resulted in increased building costs, as the tax was passed on to the consumer.

Development Land Tax, 1976–1985, had the effect of making it less financially beneficial to sell land to developers. This led to an increase in land prices, which eventually was passed on to the house buyer.

Taxation affects the industry indirectly, in that if tax rates are increased, then both private individuals and businesses have less to spend. Because the products of the industry are of a durable nature, then their replacement can always be shelved.

Other policies of government

The construction industry is very prone to what is known as the 'stop–go' policy. This is not really a single policy, but is the effect of many government and possible external actions on a particularly susceptible industry. The construction industry employs about 6 per cent of the country's labour force, which produces about 6 per cent of the GDP, which is the value of all domestic goods and services at their final market prices. In Chapter 7 it was also seen that the industry was responsible for 50 per cent of fixed capital formation. Because of the importance of the industry to the economy, the government often tries to regulate the economy by cutting back on construction activity, which will inevitably lead to a slowing of the money cycle, as the multiplier takes effect. Both fiscal and monetary policies could act as a regulator, but often more direct policies affect the industry.

At certain times, government cuts back on public spending, which was seen from Fig. 7.1, represented 50 per cent in 1978. Cutting back on spending, both on housing and service industries, has a devastating effect on the industry. These policies can come in many guises, from the reduction of budgets to certain sectors, such as major roadworks, local authorities, education, defence etc., to independent decisions on the refusal to allow the go-ahead of particular projects such as road schemes, town centre redevelopments, airports etc.

The construction industry is particularly susceptible to stop–go problems, for the following reasons:

(a) Products of this industry cannot be stockpiled, during periods of cutback, as can be done in some industries.
(b) Demand cannot be satisfied by distributing a limited number of products over the nation, due to the immobility of the product. This inevitably leads to greater problems in certain areas.
(c) A contractor often depends upon a few relatively large projects, a loss of only one or two contracts might lead to a dramatic reduction in turnover accompanied by cutback in staff.

There is often a time delay between the operation of government policies and their effects upon the industry; this comes about for two reasons:

222

(a) There is a long lead time on contracts, often years, which is necessary for planning, design and tendering procedures to be completed.
(b) The low level of activity at the start and finish of contracts, demonstrated by the 'S' curve of Fig. 19.1, means that as many contracts may only just have started when the 'brake' was applied by government, then these contracts will 'blossom', and hide the problem of depression for some months.

The above problems lead not only to a delay in the run-down of the industry, but also to a delay in its stimulation, when this is thought necessary.

Although the stop–go problems have been with us some time and will probably exist for a long time to come, they do cause the industry to be less efficient than if a steady workload could be depended upon, for the following reasons:

(a) Not only construction companies are affected, but also materials manufacturers. Because they do not have a steady order level, they are less inclined to invest in new plant and equipment which might have to lie idle for much of the time. This leads to the situation where obsolete inefficient plant is being used, not only on site, but also in the factories producing the materials.
(b) There is little incentive for contractors to take on the responsibility of training new operatives, only to have to lay them off again.

Fig. 19.1 Typical 'S' curve of cumulative contract payments

(c) There is difficulty in encouraging workers to enter the industry, when there is such insecurity of employment.

(d) Specialist service functions to the industry, such as architects, surveyors, even local authority building control and planning departments, may have to suffer fluctuations in staffing, as a result of these policies.

If some solution could be found whereby an even flow of work could be guaranteed, then the industry and the clients would benefit greatly. The two main political parties in Britain have differing views on the method of bringing this about.

At one time the Labour Party wanted to see a large proportion of the industry nationalised. By doing this, rationalisation would be possible, to avoid duplication of contracting establishments in a particular area. It would be possible then, in theory, to control the flow of work to the government contracting departments, which could then plan, it is hoped, over longer periods. The main fear that people have of this suggestion is that because the element of competition has been destroyed, bureaucracy will prevail and cause costs to rise excessively, as was often the case with DLOs.

The Conservative Party has a much more subtle approach. Its idea is to lower the proportion of work which results directly from government. This party generally tries to reduce public sector budgets, and at the same time give incentives to industry, and to private individuals to encourage investment in capital projects.

In the areas of services, such as water, gas, electricity, by cutting back on central government support, the payment for these services falls more heavily on the final consumer. It can be said therefore that as these areas become more and more self-financing, any construction work carried out for these authorities will be less and less dependent on central government.

In the area of public housing, greater home ownership is being encouraged with the permissible selling off of council houses, following the various Housing Acts, and again cash limits are being imposed on local authority spending in this area.

During the 1980s direct labour organisations were much reduced by the adoption of contracting out of many services, which ranged from grass cutting to redecorating and maintenance (see Tables 7.7 and 7.8).

The seesaw effect which tends to occur as a result of the different parties' alternating their terms of office obviously affects the industry. Possible clients of the industry are reluctant to invest in capital projects, where unknown policies may be introduced affecting them. Again if there is uncertainty about the level of forthcoming interest rates, speculation will not occur.

Sometimes the implementation of policies which might generally seem detrimental to the economy can bring benefits to the constuction industry. One such example was the introduction of the new business rating system known as the national non-domestic rate (NNDR) in the early 1990s. With this system landlords had to pay 50 per cent of the rate on an unfurnished building. If a certain amount of decommissioning were to take place the building could be taken off the rating list so that no rates were payable. This decommissioning involves virtually gutting a building, possibly taking out floor and ceiling finishes and services, but even so many landlords have contemplated this action, for if the office block were to remain unlet for several years, it would be more economical to decommission and eventually reinstate than to pay the rates.

This last chapter may seem somewhat pessimistic, but remember, there will always be a need for a construction industry. The choices open to it in the next few years are: firstly, can it stabilise its workload to enable higher efficiencies and reductions of costs? Secondly, how will the industry cope with new technologies? Will the building of the future still be semi-traditional, or will construction go to the other extreme, with all buildings being on a prefabricated modular basis, manufactured in one, or a few nationalised factories?

Questions

1 Discuss present government policies overall, in relation to their effects on the construction industry.
2 Answer again question 5 from Chapter 1. Has your answer changed at all?

Glossary of economic terms

Accelerator principle: States that changes in the demand for consumer goods cause greater changes in the demand for durable capital equipment used for their manufacture.

Agrarian Revolution: The second half of the eighteenth century, during which time a large increase took place in the efficiency of farming.

Balance of payments: This shows the summary of one country's payments to, and receipts from, other countries, during international trading, for all goods and services.

Balance of trade: Also known as the visible balance. A summary of one country's payments to, and receipts from, other countries, for dealings in actual goods.

Bilateral trade: International trading between two countries only, where each pair of countries balances its trading transactions.

Bill of Exchange: An unconditional order in writing addressed by one person to another, signed by the person giving it, requiring the person to whom it is addressed to pay on demand, or at a stated future date, a sum of money to a certain person, or to the order of that person, or to bearer.

Birth rate: The number of births, per thousand of population.

Budget: An estimate of the government's income and expenditure for the coming year, usually presented in early April.

Capital: In economic terms, means those goods used for the production of others. In financial terms it is the monetary value of real assets.

Capital gains tax: The tax payable on the realised increase in value of certain assets.

Capitalism: A political, economic system based on the making of profit by free-enterprise activities.

Capital transfer tax: A tax on the transfer of wealth, both during one's lifetime, or at death. It replaces estate duty.

Clearing house: An institution where indebtedness between various organisations is settled.

Command economy: Otherwise known as a planned economy. A system where all planning is carried out by the state.

Communism: A political and economic system, where the state formulates and implements all economic policies.

Corporation tax: A tax on company profits.

Cost—benefit analysis: A technique for evaluating several alternative solutions, particularly taking into account social costs and benefits.

Cost push inflation: Inflation induced and sustained by rising production costs.

Death rate: The number of deaths per thousand of population.

Debentures: These are securities issued by companies for long-term loans that carrry fixed rates of interest.

Deflation: A reduction of the economic activity of a nation.

Demand: The amount of a commodity that will be purchased at a particular price.

Demand pull inflation: Inflation induced by higher incomes causing higher demand, i.e. too much money chasing too few goods.

Depreciation: An allowance for the reduction in the value of an asset, due to wear and tear.

Devaluation: Is the reducing of the value of one currency in terms of another.

Direct taxation: A tax that is levied on income, e.g. income tax.

Discount house: A financial institution that discounts Bills of Exchange.

Division of labour: Where workers in a production situation specialise on one particular task.

Dumping: The selling of goods abroad, cheaper than they are sold in the home market.

Durable goods: Goods which give utility over a fairly long period, e.g. furniture, motor cars, production machinery.

Elasticity: The measure of the change in either demand or supply due to a given change in price.

Entrepreneur: The organising factor in production. The risk-taking and decision-making function.

Equilibrium: A situation where economic forces are in balance.

European community: Consists of twelve countries: Belgium, Denmark, France, Germany, Greece, Italy, Ireland, Luxembourg, The Netherlands, Portugal, Spain and the United Kingdom. They have joined together to eliminate obstacles to the free movement of goods, services, capital and labour.

Exchange rate: The rate at which one currency is exchanged for another.

External economies: Also known as 'economies of scale', economies of large-scale production of an industry.

Fiduciary issue: An issue of banknotes backed by government securities rather than by gold.

Fixed costs: The costs of a firm which do not change with variation of output in the short term.

Free economy: An economy where there is no interference by the state.

Free trade: Is international trade carried on without the imposition of any quotas or tariffs.

Gilt-edged securities: Securities which carry very little risk, often restricted to government stocks.

Gross domestic product (GDP): The value of goods and services produced within a country, but excluding net income from abroad.

Gross national product (GNP): As GDP, including any net income from abroad, but excluding money earned by overseas investment in this country.

Hedging: Action taken to protect a business or asset against changes in price.

Homogeneous product: A product which is completely identical with all others.

Horizontal integration: The expansion of a firm to give it greater capacity to carry out a single activity.

Indirect taxation: Taxes on goods or services, e.g. VAT.

Industrial Revolution: The period of about 1760 to 1850 during which the factory system replaced the domestic system of manufacture.

Inflation: A situation where prices are rising: slowly − creeping inflation; fast − galloping or hyperinflation.

Infrastructure: Capital that is invested in the transportation, communication and services networks of a country.

Internal economies: Economies which a single firm can create by expanding output.

Investment: The actual production or acquisition of capital goods. In financial terms it means the purchase of shares or securities.

Issuing house: A financial institution which specialises in raising capital for companies by organising new issues of shares.

Joint stock company: Also known as a limited company. A business organisation where the capital is divided into small parcels, known as shares, or blocks of stock. The shareholders enjoy the advantage of limited liability.

Laissez-faire: An economic political doctrine that believes State intervention in industry should be kept to a minimum.

Limited liability: Usually applied to shareholders of a limited company, where their liability is limited to the fully paid up value of the shares they hold.

Liquidity: The ease with which assets can be turned into money.

M_1: Is known as the narrow definition of money, in that it includes only the most liquid assets. It includes cash or money in bank current accounts or other assets or securities immediately convertible to cash without notice having to be given.

M_3: Is known as the wider definition of money. It includes M_1 plus all assets that are not immediately convertible to money, i.e. those that normally earn interest such as deposit accounts at banks and building societies.

Market price: The price determined by supply and demand forces, in the short term.

Minimum lending rate (MLR): Until 1972, known as the bank rate. It is the rate at which the Bank of England will act as lender of last resort to the discount market. In practice it is the rate at which it will discount eligible bills. Now discontinued in practice.

Mixed economy: An economy that is balanced between a free and planned economy.

Money: A commodity that is acceptable to all parties likely to use it as a medium of exchange.

Monopoly: A situation where a commodity, for which there is no substitute, can only be obtained from one supplier.

Multilateral trade: International trade between many countries, where individual pairs of trading nations do not have to balance payments.

Multiplier: A multiplying constant which indicates the level of output or income derived from the investment of a certain amount of capital.

Normal price: The long-term price, where supply is adjusted to demand.

Oligipoly: A situation where there are few suppliers of a commodity.

Oligopsony: A situation where there are few buyers of a commodity.

Opportunity cost: The cost, to the individual, firm, nation or whatever, of foregone alternatives that can not now be acquired, due to a decision to carry out a specific line of action.

Optimum population: The population that, when combined with other factors of production, will result in the maximum output per worker.

Planned economy: See command economy.

Progressive tax: A system of taxation, where the rate of tax increases as the income, or whatever is to be taxed, increases.

Propensity to consume: The keenness with which a person or nation will consume goods.

Propensity to save: The keenness with which a person or nation will save.

Public sector borrowing requirement (PSBR): The expected difference between government expenditure, and government income.

Quota: Concerning international trade, it is the fixing of a maximum number of units, or maximum total value of a good, to be allowed into the country over a period of time.

Real income: The value of income based upon the goods and services it will buy.

Regressive tax: A tax which is not related to a person's ability to pay it. It is a tax which falls heavily on the lower paid.

Regulator: The term applied to changing of policies and taxes, to fit a given economic situation.

Shadow prices: Calculated prices or values that cannot be obtained from a market situation. Often used in cost−benefit analysis.

Single-use goods: These are non-durable goods such as food, fuel and tobacco.

Stock exchange: A market for dealing in stocks and shares, in which business can only be transacted by members.

Subsidy: A government grant to industry, or for any particular goods or service.

Substitute: Two goods could be said to be substitutes, if a rise in price of one, followed by a fall in demand directly causes a rise in demand for the other.

Supply: The quantity of a commodity that will come on to the market at a particular price, at a particular time.

Tariff: A duty or tax, imposed on imports.

Trade cycle: The regular fluctuations of business activity.

Treasury bills: These are issued by the government and are a means of obtaining short-term finance, usually three months, for the government.

Utility: The utility of a good can be said to be the degree of satisfaction a person can obtain from owning it.

Value: A good's ability to be changed for other goods.

Value added tax (VAT): A general tax added at each stage of production or exchange, on goods and services, as defined by the tax, from primary industry right through to consumption.

Variable cost: Costs which vary directly with output.

Vertical integration: Combination of firms, so that they carry out all stages of production of a commodity, from primary, through secondary processes.

Wants: Desires for commodities or services.

Weighting: A system of giving greater emphasis to certain items in a list used for compiling an index.

Yield: The relationship between the current return and current value of an investment or security.

Index